THE ULTIMATE FUNDRAISING
CASE STUDY

12 Swipe-Ready,
Real World Lessons Even the
Smallest Nonprofits Can Use
to Raise Big Money

Dan Magill

© 2017 ProActive Content All rights reserved. No part of this publication may be reproduced, distributed, or transmitted in any form or by any means, including photocopying, recording, or other electronic or mechanical methods, without the prior written permission of the publisher, except in the case of brief quotations embodied in critical reviews and certain other noncommercial uses permitted by copyright law.
ISBN (Print) 978-1-54391-025-4 (Ebook) 978-1-54391-026-1

Table of Contents

About the Author	ix
Preface – What to Expect From This Book	xi
The Story of Hetauda House	xv
Lesson 1: You Never Know What's Gonna Work	1
It Begins With Ideas – And You Can't Have Too Many	3
The Hetauda House Campaign Launches	6
Uncertainty and Regrouping	7
Our Lowest Point	8
Our Fundraising "Secret"	10
The Single Greatest Idea of the Entire Campaign	11
Lesson 1 Fundraising Takeaway	15
Lesson 2: Don't Put All Your Files on One Hard Drive	17
This was Our 'Hard Drive'	18
Lesson 2 Fundraising Takeaway	20
Lesson 3: The Absolute Necessity of Investing in Support Systems	22
Rescuing the Project Manager from the Precipice	23
Salsa's Donor and Campaign Management Tools	25
Lesson 3 Fundraising Takeaway	29
Lesson 4: Paid Workers Get It Done	
Volunteers Support the Paid Workers.	31
Lesson 4 Fundraising Takeaway	36
Lesson 5: Quality Volunteers are Priceless – Do Not Neglect Them	39
Traits of All-Star Volunteers	41
Lesson 5 Fundraising Takeaway	42
Lesson 6: Do not Leave Big Decisions to People without Expertise	45
Identifying and Gaining Fundraising Expertise	46
Why Expertise Must Be Given Decision-Making Authority	47
What Do We Do?	48

The Baker, the Runner, and the Unclear Website	49
How A Fundraising Expert Thinks About…	50
What Do We Say?	55
Lesson 6 Fundraising Takeaway	60

Lesson 7: Producing a Successful Event is a Lot Harder than It Looks   64

Hetauda Heirs of Hope Event	65
The Final Tally – Was It Worth It?	68
Event Lessons Learned – How Much More Could We Have Raised?	68
Your Expanded Auction Fundraising Guide	
How Silent Auctions Work	76
How Much Should We Charge For Our Event?	84
How Can Low Income People Be Part of Our Event?	86
Lesson 7 Fundraising Takeaway	92

Lesson 8: Have a Network You Can Tap   94

Lesson 8a: You Will Be Shocked at Some of the People Who <u>Don't</u> Give   96

Lesson 8 Fundraising Takeaway	98

Lesson 9: Get a Social Media EXPERT   99

Influence, Not Use	100
Social Media Expert Qualifications	102
Reasons Not to Use College Students, Interns, or Volunteers for Social Media	104
Social Media Is Modern Day Customer Service	105
Social Media Fundraising	106
Lesson 9 Fundraising Takeaway	109

Lesson 10: Organizational Issues *Cannot* Be Allowed to Interfere with Fundraising   111

Issue #1: No Contract	112
Issue #2: Companies Dropping Out	114
Issue #3: No Construction Budget	115

- Issue #4: Cross-Continental Communications ... 118
- Lesson 10 Fundraising Takeaway ... 122

Lesson 11: No Substitute for Thorough, Clearly Presented Information ... 124
- What Do We Have? ... 126
- Clear Information Rule #1: Do It in the Right Order ... 127
- A Graphic Design Commentary – Design is not Information ... 128
- How Bad Design Affects the Donor ... 130
- A Helpful Perspective on Web Design ... 133
- Clear Information and Big Donors ... 134
- Trust, Clarity, and Emotion ... 135
- Is Good Storytelling Enough? ... 137
- Real Example: Peer-2-Peer Ambassadors Need Something to Say ... 138
- Information Is Power ... 139
- Stories + Clear Information = Fundraising Success? ... 141
- Our Success Story Is Built Upon Clearly Presented Information ... 142
- Lesson 11 Fundraising Takeaway ... 143

Lesson 12: Have a Skilled Copywriter Create or Advise on All Donor Communications ... 146
- Why You Need a Copywriting Specialist ... 149
- But How Do I Find a Fundraising Copywriter? ... 154
- How Can I Tell if a Copywriter Is Actually Any Good? ... 155
- Why Your Fundraising Director Is Not a Copywriter ... 158
- Lesson 12 Fundraising Takeaway ... 159

Final Thoughts on the Hetauda House Building Project ... 162
- Special Fundraising Opportunity ... 170

About the Author

DAN MAGILL IS A PROFESSIONAL COPYWRITER AND MARKETING CONSULTANT, and a fundraising marketing expert. He works with nonprofits as well as businesses to help them grow their revenues, generate more leads and new donors, and nurture and develop relationships with existing customers and donors through direct response copywriting and marketing.

Dan has written emails, SEO blog and website content, sales and landing pages, lead generation content such as eBooks and opt-in pages, case studies, direct mail, event marketing, and more. He has helped launch fledgling nonprofits and worked with established ones to help them grow.

He works as both an implementer and a strategist, able to create marketing plans for clients and then implement them with written content that always puts the donor (or customer) first. Dan believes in doing what works, not what's popular or trendy, and though he works within technology as a necessary part of his craft, he is suspicious about its long term benefits for our world. In his words, "It's supposed to save us time, and yet everyone today is far busier than they were even 20 years ago."

Dan had the honor of being the principal copywriter for all the marketing content produced for the successful Hetauda House campaign. He continues to work with Friends of WPC Nepal, the organization that uses the Hetauda House now that it's been built, as well as other nonprofits around the world.

And while he also writes marketing and copy for businesses, his primary desire is to devote all his time to helping nonprofits that do humanitarian work raise the funds they need to successfully accomplish their world-changing missions. He cares about justice, freedom, empowerment, goodness, and mercy, and has little patience for apathy, cynicism, and myopic thinking.

In addition to his copywriting work, Dan has developed a talent for screenwriting. Before this, he worked as a high school teacher for many years, and still hopes to one day write the book that will set people straight about education.

He's married to his wonderfully talented wife Sarah, and has watched his world turn upside down and his emotions come alive in new ways through his delightful 2-year old son.

Preface –
What to Expect From This Book

THIS BOOK IS LIKE A SUPER-SIZED FUNDRAISING CASE STUDY. IT GIVES YOU 12 practical lessons learned that you can use immediately to launch new fundraising campaigns or scale up your existing ones.

These lessons come to you from the triumphant Hetauda House campaign, which raised $475,000 in ten months on a shoestring budget to build a new human trafficking safe home in Nepal.

It has been written for one audience primarily, but perhaps we can stretch it to two.

To anyone who wants to get better at fundraising, this book is for you. And since I can't imagine anyone involved in nonprofit fundraising who doesn't think they can get better, it's for anyone who works in fundraising, in any capacity. This applies to seasoned workers at established nonprofits, frazzled and overworked staffers and volunteers at smaller and newer charities, and people who want to do something for the benefit of others but are overwhelmed at where to begin.

Even if you're just one person and not part of any organization, and want to raise $10,000 to help a friend, this book will help you.

Fundraising is hard, and there is no sugar-coating in this book. I make no promises about things that are "guaranteed" to work, because nothing is. The best copywriters and fundraisers in the world have all failed at one point or another. But you can succeed, if you take these tools and use them.

My goal with this book is twofold:

1) To inspire you to believe you can do better at your fundraising
2) To give you super-practical and applicable tasks and ideas that you can inject into your fundraising strategy, in some cases immediately

They say the best way to learn is to do. That's true. But the second best way to learn is to watch someone else do it, and learn from their mistakes and successes. That's what this book is for you. It's your chance to learn from us. Take what worked for us, and apply it to your fundraising. Observe the pitfalls we fell into, and avoid them. And since some pitfalls can't be avoided, equip yourself through our example so you will navigate them with success.

Reading this will spare you from a lot of wasted time learning hard lessons others have already learned, so you can devote more precious resources to the many other tasks on your plate.

Each chapter offers a new Lesson learned by one or more of the people who worked on the Hetauda House campaign. Some of these Lessons I already knew, but saw them play out in ways I never had before. And others I learned for the first time. There are certainly other lessons we could talk about regarding fundraising, but these are the ones that arose from our Hetauda experience.

At the end of each Lesson learned you'll see a 'Fundraising Takeaway', where you'll get a concise prescription of specific ways you can apply that Lesson to your fundraising context. *I suggest reading those parts at least twice before going on to the next Lesson.*

But this isn't just about ideas and strategies.

Preface – What to Expect From This Book

I also aim to inspire you with this story, because we all need inspiration! This campaign was extremely challenging. It wore us down emotionally and physically. It broke us at various points. You'll get a big dose of this right in the first Lesson.

But hardship is a necessity to real victory, and the strength and confidence that emerge from it.

You might be going through hardships right now. You've got work you care about, with all your heart and soul, but you're struggling to get the message out so others will care enough to join you. You're losing volunteers. You can't retain your best staffers because you can't pay them enough. People you want to help are being lost because you don't have the resources.

Dignity, human worth, justice, even the very lives or deaths of people hang in the balance of what you're able to do through your fundraising. This book will revive you with a fresh wind of confidence. This confidence will come from hearing our story, and from the practical takeaways you can use later.

The Hetauda House was built to serve as a sanctuary for women and children who are rescued from human trafficking in Nepal, or who were at risk of being ensnared by it. It's a place of provision, healing, education, comfort, and empowerment through education and job training. Because of this House, life transformation is going to happen, for hundreds, probably thousands of Nepalese people in the coming years.

Your cause is equally important. And when it gets hard, sometimes you need to be reminded that what you're trying to do is still possible. Here's a quote from *Unbreakable*, one of my favorite movies, that cuts to the heart of our human condition today:

"People are starting to lose hope. It's hard for many to believe there are extraordinary things inside themselves as well as others."

Extraordinary things *are* possible. This book will remind you of that, and will re-energize you in your quest to bring about the change your organization is fighting for.

And if I could stretch the audience for this book to a second type of person, that's the one. Anyone out there who needs encouragement, but is tired of sound bites and sayings that are divorced from the hardships of the real world, will benefit from reading this book.

If that's you, some of the fundraising tips won't mean as much to you. But in the story behind them, the huge challenge we faced before we began, its doubling in size right before we launched our campaign, the repeated setbacks, failures, and defeats, and our eventual success – you will be encouraged and strengthened.

Read it. Take notes. Share your thoughts with others in your life and work. And tell me how this book helped or encouraged you in your fundraising.

You can reach me through my website at proactivecontent.net.

And as a bonus, if you're a fundraiser and feel after reading this book that you'd benefit from some outside help, there's a special limited-time offer at the end.

The Story of Hetauda House

BEFORE WE GET TO THE LESSONS, I WANT TO SHARE THE STORY OF HETAUDA. That way, we can focus on the lessons and what you can learn from them, without having to restate all the details of the charity or its history.

The story begins with a woman named Lila Ghising. She grew up in Hetauda, Nepal, uneducated and illiterate until the age of 12. With her parents unable to care for her, she ended up living with her grandmother.

As a child, she had many friends who lived in the area. But as she got older, a strange series of events began to occur, and they took on a familiar and ominous pattern. One by one, her friends would just be gone. There one day, and gone the next. She couldn't figure out why.

Sometimes she would ask their parents or whoever had been caring for them. And she'd usually be told that they'd gone to India or somewhere else to go to school or get a job. Each time she heard this, Lila was jealous, because she wasn't able to go to school, and her family was very poor.

But as she got older, she realized how much her grandmother had protected her. She eventually discovered the truth. She had been lied to. These friends she'd lost hadn't gone to school. They'd been trafficked. She would likely never see them again, and they were probably living in horrific conditions, if they were even still alive.

Lila eventually got in school, and excelled enough to go to college. She decided to dedicate her life to preventing other kids and women from being trafficked and exploited through prostitution and slave labor.

After great challenges, she founded a program called the Women's Protection Center of Nepal, or WPC Nepal. This program has transformed her entire community.

WPC Nepal works with government and other organizations to rescue women and kids from human trafficking. They bring kids at-risk of trafficking into their home as well. Too many kids in Nepal, especially girls, are not cared for by their parents, for a variety of reasons. Many are in low castes and are not even allowed to enter certain houses or touch other people's food. Most cannot afford school, since Nepal has no public schools.

They wander the streets. Alone. Vulnerable. Hopeless. And traffickers kidnap them. Sometimes, their own relatives even sell them. If they manage to escape their traffickers, their relatives often won't let them back in because of the shame they project upon them.

WPC Nepal takes these kids and women in. They provide good meals at regular intervals, something many of the kids have never experienced. They enroll the kids in school, and provide additional tutoring outside of school. They help them learn to trust each other, their new friends, and themselves. Most of all, they empower them by giving them a new future through education, a chance to change their nation and culture so others don't suffer as they have.

Lila started this in 2005, and some of the kids who have been there for many years are starting to show some serious ambition. They want to be principals, doctors, nurses, social workers - the kinds of people who can transform a culture and a nation.

And for the women, WPC Nepal provides job training, and gives them the tools and skills to start their own businesses, usually making and selling clothing, which is big business in Nepal. It doesn't take much for them to make a good living and provide for themselves. WPC Nepal has given over a hundred women the ability start businesses. Women who were destitute, broken, hopeless, and had no skills or future.

It's amazing work. So what's the problem?

The problems began a while ago, and continued for years. Not enough space. Unreliable rental situations. Being forced to suddenly uproot isn't easy when you need garden space and are caring for dozens of kids.

It got worse in 2015 when the big earthquakes (remember those?) flattened large portions of Nepal. Hetauda was not spared. The WPC Nepal rented facility was critically damaged. It still stands, but has cracks everywhere and is no longer safe. And it's still too small.

For years, Lila has wanted to build her own facility, a place she could own and use forever. She wanted this so badly that she paid for a plot of land many years back. But she never had the funds to build on it. So it sat there. Year after year. An empty field of dreams.

Today, now armed with a Masters degree and able to speak multiple languages, Lila has become a champion for women and kids in Nepal, a fundraiser, a networker, a translator, and so much more. She eventually moved to Seattle, WA, and founded an American fundraising branch for her organization called Friends of WPC Nepal. But she still hadn't found a way to build her permanent safe home.

In 2012, the catalyst she needed finally arrived. A group of men from Seattle had banded together with a mission to effect change for the benefit of others. They called themselves the "Go-to-Guys." When they heard Lila's story, it was exactly what they were looking for.

They went to Nepal, along with a film director, who filmed footage he would later turn into a 20 minute documentary. They met the kids and women in the home. They saw the brokenness, and witnessed profound expressions of the healing that has already taken place, and continues. They cleared the ground Lila had purchased in preparation for the home that was to be built there.

And then they returned to the US. And Hetauda House was born.

In the next couple years, blueprints were drawn. Plans were made to raise the money. A website was created. And a local church in Seattle took on the task of spearheading the creation of a 5-story facility that will house up to 60 women and kids, more than double the current number.

The same WPC Nepal program that's already working, will be able to take in many more survivors, more than doubling its impact in Hetauda and beyond.

I was not part of any of that. I have never been to Nepal. But I am part of the church where Lila met some of the key people who would go on to turn Hetauda House into a reality. And I care about human trafficking, a lot.

So in late 2014, when the campaign to raise $250,000 to build the Hetauda House for WPC Nepal was starting to come into focus, I wanted in. Right before we launched our campaign, we learned we'd need $500,000, twice as much as we'd been expecting. A bad omen?

Why it went up, and what we did about it - the rest of this book tells this story of what I learned as the copywriter and as part of the strategic fundraising team that built the Hetauda House.

Some deserving recognition of others who contributed to this campaign

Perry Burkholder - project leader, and pastor of Every Nation Church Seattle

Joanna Broussard - project manager for about 8 months

Sarah Magill - project manager for about 10 months (and a very attractive one…)

Brian Behnken - designer, photographer, videographer, and overall Hetauda champion

The Story of Hetauda House

Heidi Boon – super volunteer and go-getter with serious follow-through

Abbi Engel – selfless and risk-taking volunteer with boundless creativity

Christian St. Jacques – marketing team expert and 'Go-to-Guy'

Jason Fortman – web developer and project planner who helped save the website

Aaron Brown – web developer who created the newest and best version of the website

Kiani and Nia Pineiro-Hall – launch event coordinating team

Irene Yung – super Ambassador who raised more than any other P2P-er

Johanna Wang – super Ambassador who kept raising her goal and then surpassing it

Michelle Takashima – super Ambassador who ran her own events with total strangers

Elizabeth McCollum – super Ambassador who sold craft items and surpassed her ambitious goal

Every volunteer who gave of their time whose names I don't know or can't recall

And of course – all the donors, big and small, foundations and churches. Without you, that field would still be a field, instead of a 5-story earthquake-proof refuge for 60 women and kids.

Lesson 1

You Never Know What's Gonna Work

HOW DO YOU MOTIVATE SOMEONE TO GIVE AWAY THEIR MONEY WHEN THEY receive no material benefit?

That is _the_ question of most fundraising endeavors.

And it's one we should think long and hard about with every decision we make about fundraising. Why should people give to us?

Yet so many nonprofits and charities keep operating by the simplistic belief that all people need is to hear about our great and noble cause, and they'll give. "If people just knew…" Have you ever said that, or heard someone on your team say it? Especially when you're on the ground, in the rawness of it all?

The implication is that the work we're doing is so important, so vital, so amazing, so life-changing, so emotionally fulfilling, so transformational – how could _anyone_ not give to our campaign once they learn what we're doing??!

I added the extra '?' and '!' because people who operate under this flawed assumption find themselves utterly shocked when people don't give. Especially after how hard we worked!!!

And yet it happens so often. People hear about your cause, listen to your stories, ask questions, seem interested, even make promises to follow up. And then they vanish into thin air, without a trace. It happened on the Hetauda House campaign, many more times than I can count. This is lesson 0: *Fundraising is hard.*

Lesson 1 is first because it's the foundational lesson of fundraising, and I'll get to it in a bit. But before we get to Lesson 1, you first must accept this "Lesson 0" axiom. It's a truth about people, and it's the pre-requisite to learning all the lessons in this book. And if you don't or can't accept it, none of the other lessons in this book will produce the value that they otherwise would. Here's the clearest way I can say it:

Lesson 0: No one has to give anything to your cause. Ever. Even after you make the most impassioned and emotional and gut-wrenching and beautiful and professional appeal. They do not have to give.

You can't make them do it. They have to want to do it.

Perhaps just as important to accept is that they aren't bad people if they don't give. People have budgets. Other priorities. Other things they care about. Not enough time. Caring is hard, and not just on the wallet.

No one has to give, get involved, tell their friends, share your posts, read your emails, sign up for your newsletter, or volunteer. They don't have to view your photos, or listen to your podcasts, or watch your videos. They don't have to reply to your letters. And their refusal to do any of those things doesn't mean they're selfish. They're people. Not numbers in a database. Think of them with the same respect you'd give anyone walking down the street.

This is where we begin. Because the story you're about to hear is visceral, filled with people who didn't give to us, even though we would have sworn under oath that they would. I'll be exposing mistakes, frustrations, biases, and disappointments. But I'll also be commending our successes, wisdom, perseverance, and professionalism. Because we succeeded. We met our goal. And the Hetauda House is nearly finished being built as I write this.

You're about to learn from the journey we took for Hetauda House, through all the highs and lows, of which there were plenty of both. By the end, I hope you feel encouraged, equipped, more aware, and just plain smarter. And I hope the lessons we learned become the lessons you learn as you apply them to your fundraising context.

And if that's the case, I'd love to hear from you. Just send me a quick email to copydan@proactivecontent.net

It Begins With Ideas – And You Can't Have Too Many

When we started the Hetauda House campaign, we had a healthy handful of ideas. Working on any type of marketing campaign – be it fundraising, sales, lead generation, or something else – you'll hear a lot of ideas. Part of the skill is in identifying the ones with the most promise of return and that you can accomplish without burning out your resources. (Note: Your resources are time, money, personnel, and materials).

In other words, suppose someone brings you a fundraising idea, and it takes a few hours to implement. Later, you learn that idea led to $500 in donations.

Then, suppose there's another idea that requires several people and dozens of hours to make happen. And that idea leads to $1000.

In terms of the health of your organization, the second idea is a failure. 80 hours of work from multiple people to produce $1000 isn't worth it – even if they're volunteers (*especially* if they're volunteers, actually). Because if you had devoted all those hours and people to something more effective, you would have produced far more in return.

The problem is, if you're a small campaign – or even worse, a one-time campaign like we were – then you have very few paid staff, hardly any volunteers, and no systems in place. That makes it really hard to judge what you should be doing.

That's the situation we found ourselves in for most of the Hetauda House campaign. As a result – we tried just about everything we could make happen. By my count, we implemented at least 23 different ideas over the course of ten months. And that doesn't count the ones we tried but never completed, or the many more ideas attempted by various Hetauda Ambassadors – our peer to peer fundraising branch. (We'll talk more about Ambassadors in a later chapter).

As one of the leaders of this campaign, I got to observe dozens of ideas go from the initial proposal through various stages of development. I saw where they stalled, what gave people the greatest difficulty, how it looked from the administration side – everything.

At least 11 of the fundraising ideas we executed ended up as failures.

At least 12 of them I count as successes.

Those are some really sobering statistics – and not ones I see talked about in most fundraising circles.

If you expect to raise a large sum of money, and pin all your hopes on one strategy, you're doomed. Like crowdfunding. People go all ga-ga over online tools these days, and crowdfunding hit the world by storm a few years ago. But crowdfunding was mainly created as a means for individuals, not established organizations, to raise money.

We did zero crowdfunding for Hetauda House. We considered it. We looked into it. But the fees you have to pay, the restrictions the various sites impose, and the questionable nature of its effectiveness when combined with everything else we were already doing with our limited resources and manpower – we decided it wasn't worth it.

And boy am I glad. And I'm not saying crowdfunding is a losing strategy. Like any idea, it depends on a lot of questions and variables. The biggest one is – what's your dollar amount goal, and is a crowdfunding site going to reach the size of the audience you'll need to reach that goal.

If it's a big goal, the answer is, not likely. Crowdfunding for big dollar amounts depends on two main components to be successful – a large and generous network, and a viral effect. If you're missing either of those and want to raise big money ($10,000 is not big. $500,000 is), you will likely fall short, and be left wondering what else you could have done.

No one can predict when something will go viral. If your fundraising campaign relies on something going viral – you are setting yourself up to fail. It's very difficult to just "dream up" a viral campaign. Hoping for 'virality' is akin to playing the stock market by putting all your money in one company. You do need some knowledge of how the system works, but all this does is get you in the game. It can never guarantee a winner. It's mostly luck and timing. The internet is not the giver of effortless fundraising, though some like to tell you otherwise.

So this is Lesson 1. <u>You don't know what's going to work</u>. You don't. Neither does the guy next to you who "knows" crowdfunding is the best strategy, like, ever. If you try only one strategy, and it fails, then you've failed. But if you try lots of ideas, like we did, and half of them fail (half!), you can still succeed.

For us, we still fell into the trap of relying too much on one strategy, at first. In our case, it wasn't crowdfunding. It was a documentary filmed in Nepal before the campaign began. See Lesson #2 for more details about what we learned from that.

I and others noticed this flaw right when we came on board, and worked quickly to correct it by introducing multiple facets and tools to the plan before we launched the campaign. By the time we finally launched, we had a real plan.

Here are ten of the strategies we used when our campaign began:

1) Use a documentary to tell the story of Hetauda House, and get people to watch it on the website.
2) Create a peer-to-peer Ambassador program, which empowers supporters to go out and raise funds from their own networks – people we could never otherwise reach.
3) Activate our own networks. One person on our team was connected with a large network of churches, and he worked tirelessly to get them to support Hetauda House.
4) Broaden the reach of the website. This was my primary emphasis when the campaign launched. The original site was a failure before we even started, for a host of reasons you'll read about in Lesson #12.

5) Create a newsletter to capture people and keep them updated on how things are going. Tie this to the website and any in-person events.

6) Purchase a CRM donor management program. We used Salsa Labs, a nonprofit niche CRM. Many lessons were learned through this experience, as you'll see in Lesson #4. We <u>would not</u> have met our goal in ten months without this.

7) Hold a campaign launching fundraising event.

8) Write a letter to businesses to win their support.

9) Write letters to influencers in the anti-human trafficking community (we hoped this would help our campaign go viral).

10) Apply for a grant from a foundation someone on our team had a connection with.

The Hetauda House Campaign Launches

Now remember – I said we tried at least 23 ideas over the course of this campaign. Why so many? Because we started in September 2015 with these ten, hoping to raise all the money by the end of the year, less than four months later. An ambitious goal, to say the least.

When January 1st, 2016 arrived, how much had we raised? Around $200,000. We needed $500,000.

Not good.

What happened? Quite simply, ideas 1, 8, and 9 failed, and ideas 2, 3, 4, 5, and 6 succeeded to a degree, but not nearly at the level we had hoped.

This was especially true with the Ambassador program. Our tagline for this was, "If 500 people raise $1000 each, the Hetauda House will be built." 500 people doesn't seem like very many. And the average amount raised per Ambassador, by the end, turned out to be around $1000. The problem? We only got 35 Ambassadors. And most of them came on after January 1st.

I still consider this program one of our successes. $35,000 is nothing to be sad about. But it was a lot harder to make happen than some people thought it would be. Why was it so difficult? You already know the main reason: Because <u>no one</u> has to give money to your cause, no matter how great you think it is. And being an Ambassador takes commitment. It's a lot easier to just write a check.

By the end of 2015, we had tried several more strategies in addition to those original ten. Most of those had failed too.

Our failures were mounting, volunteers were getting sapped, project funds were running out, and networks were almost tapped out.

Uncertainty and Regrouping

So we found ourselves in, quite honestly, a pretty discouraged and uncertain place. We felt like we had tried everything, and we weren't even halfway to meeting the need. So what did we do? We held a team meeting, and just brainstormed. We tossed in all kinds of ideas. Nothing was off the table. Probably over 30 real ideas got their time in the sun.

Here are a few of the ones we implemented as a result of this meeting:

1) Partner with Nepali and Indian restaurants, and ask them to give a portion of the proceeds from one day's business to Hetauda House
2) Present at a local arts and music house that features a nonprofit each month
3) Increase our social media strategy with two tactics. Actively promote Hetauda to our networks, and seek new supporters with "boosted" posts on Facebook
4) Design a Hetauda House T-shirt and sell it online
5) Empower one of our friends who had good relationships with some big-pocketed business leaders, so he can pitch them for support
6) Find more grants to apply for

Guess what happened when we implemented these ideas? More failures! Four of these six ideas failed too, some of them miserably.

The Facebook plan had positive effects and paid off later, so that was a success. And the restaurant idea succeeded as well, but it was a small amount of actual dollars. But the other four?

For how much time it took, the T-shirt idea was a disaster. We did sell some shirts, but in total this brought in less than $1000, and it took volunteers an *enormous* amount of time to create them, because the design was highly original. It was a ton of work, and just didn't pay off for the time invested.

The local arts presentation? 200 people heard a 5-minute pitch and saw one of our video trailers. Not bad exposure, right? We made 48 bucks. We stood there watching people toss tens and twenties at the beer man, including generous tips, even though it was bottled and all he had to do was reach behind himself and grab one. But they walked right by our little group and the table we had arrived early to set up. Apparently for these people, beer is more important than sex-trafficked children in Nepal. I mean, how could they not give??!! We should have guilt-tripped them more!!! (There's that excessive punctuation again....*no one has to give.*)

And that friend with deep pocketed business ties? He turned us down.

The new grants we applied for? All of them flopped. It turns out, hardly any grants like to fund capital construction projects. Go figure. And the ones that do - you might spend dozens of hours filling out all their little forms, answering their questions, and then forcing it to fit into their totally unrealistic page limits, only to still be rejected. We were. Every time. And with volunteer labor doing most of this soul-crushing grunt work, you can only do it so many times.

Our Lowest Point

By the end of February, things had gone from bad to worse. Some money that had been pledged or given earlier had finally been verified (our accountant wasn't very communicative), so we were now hovering around $250,000. But now, truly, we were out of ideas.

Our little brainstorming session hadn't produced many returns for all our hard work, and time was now becoming an increasingly fearsome factor, casting an enlarging shadow over our flailing efforts. This was a limited-time campaign. The construction needed to begin soon, because it had to be timed around the monsoon season. We had a project manager getting ready <u>to leave for Nepal</u> in a couple weeks. Even more depressing, we had raised the amount of our original goal, before we found out the price had doubled.

Remember, the original bid estimate from 2012 was $250,000. Massively increased construction costs led to a doubling of that when we updated the bids a month before we launched the campaign in 2015. Not a very good sign at the time, but we went ahead undeterred. Had that price increase not happened, we would be done.

As it was, we were only halfway, but were completely out of ideas.

To make matters worse, the bidding process for the construction contract in Nepal was dragging out and turning into a total fiasco. Bidders were dropping out. Contract details kept changing. Terrible communication across the ocean led to more delays. (You'll learn more about this drama in Lesson #10).

So, not only had we raised just half the money, we didn't even know for sure what the final costs would be! We were asking people to give to a project that still had no construction bid or final budget, and we had to keep our supporters and donors motivated and positive, without lying to them.

This was our lowest point.

Money was trickling in, but there was no way we'd raise another $250,000 by June 30th, our revised (for the third time) campaign end-date.

So what did we do?

We kept working. We found fresh life with a couple new volunteers who fortunately were unemployed and had plenty of time to help. (That tells you something about relying too much on volunteers – listen to the hidden truth in that statement – more on this in Lesson #4).

We kept writing emails.

Posting on Facebook.

Encouraging our Ambassadors.

Making fresh appeals to our dwindling list of untapped networks.

Taking any and every new volunteer who came our way with an idea.

And then, something amazing happened in the month of April.

Our Fundraising "Secret"

And this is the part you need to hear. This is why you keep doing the things you *know* will work, given enough time. The proven things, tested by decades of precedent. This is why you keep sending emails, keep talking about your campaign, keep posting, and keep trying.

When you stay at the front of people's minds, you are nurturing future supporters. This is true of for-profit marketing as well as nonprofit. With **potential** donors, if you want to turn them into **actual** donors, you have to make them care about your cause. You have to persist. You have to *invade* their routines. Conquer their minds so they think about you.

The thing is, you don't even know they're thinking about you, necessarily. But they are. And when the time comes, when they have a chance to do something, some of them will blow your mind.

In April, our campaign received a major gift of $50,000. In one swoop. The amazing thing was, this person didn't have this money until now, because of a large transaction that had recently happened. But this person chose, out of great love and generosity, to give this desperately-needed amount to Hetauda House.

And that's something that every fundraising professional needs to stop and ponder over. This person's first reaction after receiving a large infusion of money was to give a huge portion of it to Hetauda House. Before all the other things they could have done with it. How could something like this happen?

Do you understand your donors? If you do, then you know why someone would make a financial choice of this magnitude. The only way to get this kind of spontaneous and unexpected gift is to work for it. And all the work we had done before April began to pay off in this moment.

This is why the email campaign, the social media campaign, the website, and some of the other ongoing efforts we'd been putting forth are all successes. Massive ones. Because if we hadn't done those things, this person wouldn't have given this huge gift. Hetauda wouldn't have been on the mind. But because we put ourselves out there, the stories and information this person had read and watched were simmering in the heart:

The faces of women and children living in the existing safe home in Hetauda. The walls and ceilings cracked from the earthquake the year before. The kids they've had to turn away because there's not enough room. The incredible story of Lila Ghising, the founder of the Nepali program, WPC Nepal, and how she grew up watching her friends disappear - there one day, gone the next - because insidious human traffickers took them to India promising school, but lying through their teeth.

We showed videos of real children living in the safe home. These videos revealed what life was like for these kids before they found refuge in the WPC safe home. Terrible stories, but all with happy endings. We called these "Stories of Hope," because each one showed the astonishing transformation these formerly abused and unwanted children experienced once they lived in the safe home for long enough.

All this work - this was on this donor's mind, even if unaware of how it got there.

This donor believed the WPC program works, because we proved it. This donor didn't hesitate to give, because of complete confidence in the impact such a large gift would produce for hundreds of future survivors.

And so - our work had paid off. We had won someone's heart. And when life circumstances turned unexpectedly, this donor acted on behalf of Hetauda.

The Single Greatest Idea of the Entire Campaign
Why do you need a fundraising professional on your team?

Because of moments like this. What does a straggling campaign do with a sudden, amazing, and unexpected gift of $50,000?

If you're feeling the vibe, and understand where we were at this point in our campaign, then you can imagine what a waterfall of life this gift felt like. But what do we do with it? How do we share this outstanding news with our donors and supporters?

<u>This is absolutely critical.</u>

There are many ways we could have shared it. Announce it on email. Social media. In person, through supporters and Ambassadors. We could have made a special video. And we also could have done all those things together. But we didn't do any of that, and the donor is still anonymous.

What we did instead was use it as a matching grant. Matching grants are a proven fundraising technique. Our donor wanted to do something like this too, *but didn't know how to sell it*. That job was entrusted to us.

And our team delivered, in the clutch, when it counted the most. This was The Idea. When this opportunity came, we were ready for it. We even had a new website, having finally dispelled of the old hard-to-use one with the help of a couple volunteers. Our new site made it much easier to enact our plan.

Our plan had two basic components: We would use the $50,000 for a matching gift campaign. And it would be a <u>limited-time</u> campaign.

Now, there's nothing ground-breaking about that idea if you've done any marketing. But knowing about great ideas has no value if you never use them. Even more, you have to know *when* to use them.

Had we been doing matching campaigns for every sizable gift that came in, then this one wouldn't have had as much value. It's just like crying wolf. Some nonprofits send out a constant stream of desperate pleas, matching gifts, and new goals to reach that it just gets tiresome. Doesn't anything good ever happen? Why should I care about this matching gift when you'll just have another one next month?

We hadn't done that. We did one matching grant early in the campaign, because the foundation that awarded us our only grant wanted it that way. But we met half of their matching just from our launch event, so we didn't have to fundraise all of it on our own. By April, that was a distant memory.

But now, the coming month of May was prime-time for matching and rhyme. Yes, I'm serious. Rhyme. Because it rolls off the tongue when done well. We launched a "50k Matching in May" campaign. One month to raise $50,000 to match this generous gift from an anonymous donor.

And we met the goal - over $55,000 raised in one month. Yes! We turned $50,000 into $105,000 in just 30 days.

A few time-honored fundraising principles were operating at this point, and you need to know these if you want to raise significant amounts of money for any cause.

1) People respond to matching gifts.

They just do. Some person or foundation gives a large gift, but for the charity to claim it, the rest of us have to give too. It feels like we're giving twice as much. It's a great concept. The idea of doubling your money is easy to understand, and very powerful.

2) People respond to deadlines.

Any marketer knows this. It's available only for a limited time. We milked this in the extreme in May of 2016. If you want to double your gift, you <u>must</u> give it during May. One couple gave a huge gift out of the profits from their house sale. Many others gave who had not yet given anything during the campaign. The deadline and the matching worked in tandem to bring out a lot more donors.

3) The end is near.

Just a matching gift and a deadline wouldn't have been enough had we done this in October. In fact, with our first matching grant, it took quite a while to match it, even with half of it raised at the launch event. One reason is because we didn't have a deadline. But the other reason is this one - it was too early. Here's what I mean:

In a campaign to raise $500,000, when you're at $74,345, it's hard to get excited. It feels like you're a long way off. Deep down, you're wondering if it's really going to happen. Where's all that money going to come from?

But when you've raised $300,000, and you know that if enough people work together to give $50,000, that this will double and now suddenly you'll be at $400,000 - now <u>that's</u> exciting.

Giving increases as you close in on your goal. It's called *momentum*. This is a fundraising axiom. But - it only happens if you make it happen. If you leverage the power of this truth.

So our great idea wasn't the matching grant. It was the combination of that with a deadline, and using language that capitalizes on the momentum this would represent - *look how close we'll be to reaching the goal if we match this!*

People responded.

It started slow. In the first week of May, we'd only seen a couple thousand come in. But on the final day of the month, when we were still a bit short, donors gave $9227. In one day! That's momentum. And it had built up not just that month, but from the whole year.

Many of these donors, as I said, had never given since the inception of the campaign, but they had been hearing about it. They were reading the emails. Watching the videos. Hearing people talk about it.

As the end of May neared, they couldn't hold back any longer. The final amount raised that month was $55,165. And just like that, we were around $400,000.

And as May came to a close, all this momentum didn't just hit a peak. It exploded like bubbles out of a champagne bottle. Not only did that $55,000 come in, but another donor, who also had a surprising turn of life events, decided to give *another* $50,000!

So not only did the first $50k get matched. But a second $50k came in as the month of May came to a close. Again - that's the power of momentum. It's what people do when they've been emotionally engaged for a while, and now they see a chance to finish the task.

We spent a year engaging emotions. We won the hearts of a lot of these people over the previous nine months. But now, with the end in sight, they just exploded in generosity.

With June 30th as our final end date, we still needed another $30,000 or so, but it just felt easy by that point. We knew it would happen now. The beast had been slain. The victory was ours. All that remained was to collect the spoils.

Lesson 1 Fundraising Takeaway

This was our journey. No two fundraising journeys will be the same. But I hope you see the lesson learned here. If I can state it now in a positive, activist manner, I would say it like this:

Do lots of ideas.

Some of your ideas will fail. Expect it. Even the ones you thought were the best.

Other ideas will succeed. And still others will surprise you and produce far more than you expected. And remember – not every idea is about money, necessarily. Keeping people engaged is really important. It's absolutely vital. So an idea that engages people with your story and keeps your cause on the forefront of their minds, even if they aren't giving much at the time, is still a good idea.

The only limitations on the ideas you can do are time, money, and personnel. For small organizations like ours running a one-time campaign, all three of these worked against us.

But we had one thing in our favor – a network of people who knew the story of the Women's Protection Center in Nepal, and cared about it deeply. Those people proved to be the difference. They became the donors, the volunteers, and the Ambassadors who made it happen.

And today, the day I first wrote these words, the new Hetauda House has broken ground. All those gifts will transform the lives of hundreds of Nepalese women and kids entering the WPC Nepal program in the coming years. It was all worth it.

A final thought on ideas. Even your failures can be turned into successes. Remember that arts presentation that raised a measly $48 because some people like beer more than helping exploited children? Six one dollar bills of that $48 came from the hands of a little boy who couldn't have been more than eight years old. That kid's six dollars helped build this house.

And we told his story several times in the final months to other donors. There's little doubt it moved some people to give.

As a wise philosopher once said, "If we don't try, then we don't do." Try lots of ideas, and keep working at the ones that work. Use every tool and outcome and scrap of hope you can find, and do not restrict yourself to just a handful of ideas someone else thinks are all you'll need.

Eventually, you'll reach the finish line. But only if you're willing to do whatever it takes to go the distance.

Lesson 2

Don't Put All Your Files on One Hard Drive

YOUR PARENTS WOULD HAVE SAID THIS DIFFERENTLY. SOMETHING ABOUT EGGS in a basket. My eggs come in a cardboard carton at the grocery store, so I don't really get that one.

But if I put all my files on a single hard drive, what happens if my computer fails? Lots of unhappiness.

We all know the sayings, and yet how often do we see it done this way in fundraising (and in sales too)? We see campaigns launched whose success depends entirely on a single item. One story. One person. One advertising medium. One shot-in-the-dark gamble in hopes of a "viral" thingy.

If your entire campaign depends on a single item, then your entire campaign can fail before it begins. You need a multi-pronged approach.

Any fundraising endeavor that needs to sustain itself simply cannot be entrusted to a solitary item of content or a single strategy. If that item doesn't sell like you expected, or catch on like you were promised, then you're dead.

This was Our 'Hard Drive'

Before we began this campaign, the Hetauda House didn't exist. It was just an idea, a theory, a schematic on a piece of paper. Women and kids rescued from human traffickers can't live in a paper house. We had to raise half a million dollars, and we had to do it in less than a year.

Those kids and that house have too much at stake to entrust them to a single 20 minute documentary - especially one that can only be viewed online.

And yet - that was the original plan.

The original strategy was to drive people to a website through methods still to be determined and with the help of a peer-to-peer (P2P) fundraising program called Ambassadors. Once there, they would view the documentary, be inspired and moved by the story of Lila and her program, and then give. The success or failure of this new safe home was 100% dependent on a single 20 minute documentary.

A few problems with this:

   1) Online viewers don't like to watch long videos

Even five minutes can be pushing it. Now, this isn't true if they have been led through a strategic marketing funnel, and are now primed to want to watch the video (or read an eBook, or download a white paper, or read a long sales page, etc).

But for first-time traffic, for people hearing about your campaign for the first time, they will be hard-pressed to sit through a 20 minute documentary unless someone is holding their hand the whole way. It's just the nature of the web. People are less patient online.

So for our $250,000 campaign (which ballooned to $500,000 a month before we launched) to depend on this one piece of content was a grave error.

What will we do if people don't want to sit through the 20 minutes? We have no backup plan. No alternative way to learn about Hetauda. Nothing to post on social media other than this one content item that's 20 minutes long. The false assumption of Lesson 0 is in full view here – the underlying assumption that people will "just give" once they see a video.

2) The documentary doesn't give details.

It's a very moving documentary. Filmed on site in Nepal, it tells founder Lila Ghising's story, and introduces you to several other women and kids in the WPC Nepal program. It opens your eyes, shows you how deeply rooted this problem is in Nepal, and gives you a profound admiration for Lila.

It also makes you feel like you can do something. And that was its purpose. This video raises the questions, arrests the emotions, and makes you care. The video is an attention-getter, and a very good one. Getting people's attention is the first step in marketing.

But it doesn't tell you <u>what</u> to do after that. If I want to give, how do I do it? It also doesn't explain the new house or give any details about what it's for or why we need it. It doesn't show what it will look like, what it will cost, or why it will cost that much. In marketing terms, this video isn't going to close the sale. It's just not made for that.

The only people who will give based solely on seeing this documentary are people who *already know* about the program, or they know someone else who does and can ask them questions.

But we were going after grants. Big donors. Businesses. People who care about trafficking and have given to other organizations (why should they give to ours?). Those people aren't going to give just from this one documentary. For them, this will start the conversation and raise the issue. But it will not close the deal.

3) Can't build momentum with only one item.

Buzz. It's what every fundraising campaign wants. We want people to talk about this. We want to build momentum. Create conversation. Incite passion and awareness.

If we're going to raise $500,000 in just a few months, we don't just want momentum. We are *absolutely dependent on it*. You saw the power of momentum in Lesson #1. It's pretty hard to build any kind of momentum if all you have is a website, a documentary, and some Ambassadors. What about progress updates? What about sending out fresh waves of fundraising requests, and follow-up campaigns? What about enlisting new people who find out about us to help us reach the goal? Can you do all this without momentum?

There are a lot of strategies that fundraising campaigns can use to create and sustain momentum. Newsletters updates, events, blog posts, social media, and many others. And we needed all of them for Hetauda to become a reality.

The initial plan relied solely on one documentary. The plan that succeeded used a whole lot more. And we saw people - people who had heard about this for months - finally get excited about it and become Ambassadors. It took months for some of them to find their passion.

Why? Because we have to break in to their normal routine existence. We have to disrupt their lives. That's not something you're going to accomplish with a single video, no matter how profound it might be.

Lesson 2 Fundraising Takeaway

If all you have is one magic trick, no one's going to get excited after seeing it for the eighteenth time.

The implications for this lesson touch every aspect of marketing and fundraising. Today, too many swear by single methods and strategies and exclude all others. They abandon direct mail and email, and use only social media. Or they use Youtube videos to bring in all their new leads. Or Adwords. Or AdGrants. Or crowdfunding.

Entrusting the success of your entire campaign, or even worse, of your entire nonprofit's continuing existence, to a single strategy is unwise in the extreme. I've read stories of businesses who used Facebook to generate leads, and then Facebook altered something in their policy that disallowed their method of advertising. All in one day - no leads.

It wasn't so long ago that many sites relied exclusively on organic search and the keyword-centric version of SEO, so they stuffed hidden keywords all over their websites. When Google altered their algorithm and started penalizing this behavior, those sites went down in flames. And Google changes their algorithm constantly. What worked one year suddenly does nothing the next.

Take heed to this, if this describes your fundraising approach. If you're dependent on one source, one method, or one *person* for your success, your long term growth – and possibly your organization's very survival – is on very shaky ground.

Diversify. Broaden. Invest in multiple marketing channels and methods. Create more content. Tap new markets. Reach new audiences. Change your message, and change the way you deliver it. Will this raise your expenses a bit? Most likely. But will it keep you going when your 'favorite' source of donations or supporters suddenly vanishes? Most certainly.

Lesson 3

The Absolute Necessity of Investing in Support Systems

ONCE WE HAD A PLAN THAT INVOLVED MORE THAN TRUSTING A 20-MINUTE DOC-umentary to spark a viral donation bonanza (which it didn't), we encountered a new problem. How will we administer and manage this multi-pronged fundraising campaign? Who will do it? How long will it take them each week?

Here's a rundown of just some of the tasks *someone* would have to make happen:

- Run a peer-to-peer fundraising campaign – our Ambassador program
- Send a regular online newsletter
- Conduct in-person presentations to our networks and churches
- Facilitate in-person presentations by people not directly connected to us, such as Ambassadors and advocates who lead other churches
- Collect and process online donations
- Collect and process in-person donations
- Plan the launch event and collect and process donations given there

- Track and record donations, signups, and volunteers to build long term relationships between these new supporters and the WPC Nepal program that runs in the safe home
- Support other people who strike out to attempt their own fundraising efforts
- Work with the construction project manager in Nepal

Before we launched, most of these 'to-do' items lingered way off in the distance in a big, hazy, amorphous cloud called "Stuff we'll deal with later."

As we got closer to taking the campaign public, it became pretty clear, very fast, that we'd need a whole lot more than good intentions, a documentary, a multi-pronged plan, and a project manager.

Yes, we did have a project manager, our only paid staff person at this time. And she was willing and able to do all these tasks because she loved the WPC Nepal program and wanted to work from home. But she would never be able to manage all this on her own, and certainly not in the 20 hours per week we could afford to pay her at a completely unworthy but best-we-could-do rate of payment. Not. A. Chance.

That would be borderline insanity. No one, anywhere, could have done all this. At least, not with the tools currently available to us. Here's what we had: A website, a capture form, a Paypal donate button, five loaves, and two fish.

Rescuing the Project Manager from the Precipice

As Yoda might say, "Coordinate a $500,000 campaign in four months with only these tools, you cannot."

Now, being well-read in your field is one example of an intangible asset you just can't put a pricetag on (and incidentally, one that never shows up on those "Dear Santa" job posts so many companies and nonprofits put out with absurdly valuable requirements for equally absurdly meager pay). Being well-read indicates continuous learning, another priceless intangible.

But I knew the only answer to our growing list of needs was a Customer Relationship Management system, commonly known as a CRM. As a nonprofit-focused copywriter and marketer, I had read a number of authoritative articles (content marketing – see? It works) from Salsa Labs, a nonprofit-specialist CRM that could assist us with almost everything on our to-do list. So I pursued them to confirm they had the tools we needed, got a price, and then pitched it to our project leader.

Once our team saw the demonstration of what Salsa could do, it was a no-brainer. The CRM would at least make it possible – though still highly improbable – that our project coordinator wouldn't jump off a cliff after three months on the job. Fortunately, she never did, though I have it on good authority she expelled cries of desperation, grunts of frustration, and tears of pent up despair on more than one occasion. And that was just from setting up the CRM!

So you could say, though it might be a bit of an exaggeration, that the CRM saved her life, although it certainly didn't make it a paradise.

The point here, as you've hopefully gathered, is that you cannot run a successful multi-pronged campaign to raise large amounts of money without a system in place. But setting up that system will take a lot of time, and it won't be easy.

I had a large role in setting up the Salsa account. We didn't need every feature they offer, but that didn't matter. Backend systems like this are notoriously hard to use, and this one isn't an exception. If you don't know code (like me and either of our project managers – one took a break for a few months), there are certain things you just can't do very easily.

We spent a lot of time writing to customer support to solve various problems we couldn't get around. When you want a web page to do a certain task or look a certain way, sometimes this takes a little extra attention. I can attest that I lost my patience for it several times.

But so you can see the value of having a functioning and empowering backend system, let's take a look at some of what a CRM can do for you. (And no, if you're wondering, I am not an affiliate marketer for Salsa. Just a good ol' satisfied customer).

Salsa's Donor and Campaign Management Tools

Personalized Donation Pages

One of the primary benefits of a Salsa-style CRM is the unlimited donation pages. What does that mean?

If you go look at far too many fundraising sites and visit their donation pages, you'll see what the Hetauda House site also used to have – a Paypal donate button. Let me be clear on this: If you want your campaign to fail, this is a great way to do it. Fundraising data has proven that personalized donation pages that have the same general appearance as the rest of the site, teamed up with campaign-specific copywriting and messaging, earn up to five times as much in donations than generic forms from sites like Paypal. Five times as much!

Why? Because the online world is fraught with peril and uncertainty. Who can we trust? Hardly anyone. And when you are on a site, and then you click a link and end up on a totally different site with completely altered design, you get nervous. It's a natural human reaction. A branded donation page that looks the same as the rest of your site eliminates this problem.

If you're using Paypal or something like it for you donation page, you are losing money. Buckets of it.

Why does it matter? It goes back to the timeless fundraising axiom I mentioned back in Lesson #1: No one has to give to your cause. Giving is a selfless act. If I give money away, I get a good feeling, hopefully. And that's it, most of the time. While we can do things to make this decision more enjoyable (and we should), the bottom line is, I'm not going to get anything of material substance that comes anywhere close to the value of the money I just gave away.

And especially online, where everything moves fast and is so impersonal, when a person makes a decision to give their money away, they need all the reinforcement they can get.

And a Paypal form doesn't reinforce squat.

Salsa and other nonprofit CRMs understand this. So one of their best features is customizable donation pages. Salsa offers an unlimited number of these. That means, for instance, you could create a general donation page for your main website. But you could also make a different donation page, with different copy, a different button, and different images for a Giving Tuesday micro-campaign. And you could make another one for a Christmas giving push.

You could make still another for a direct mail campaign. We didn't use direct mail, because for a one-time campaign it's not likely to be cost-effective. But if you were to send out a direct mail fundraising letter, you could put a unique URL just on that letter, and that URL could lead to a donation page that only people who see that letter can get to. Then you can make your offer specifically to them, increasing personalization, credibility, and effectiveness.

But even if you just make ONE donation page using your CRM, it's still five times more valuable than your generic Paypal page with all those ugly fields and no reinforcing messaging.

And that's just one benefit of a CRM.

Peer-to-Peer Fundraising Tools

We also ran our entire Ambassador program through Salsa. Before having Salsa, there was really no plan for how to do this. You're talking about lots of forms, databases, Excel sheets, and very complicated record keeping. If a donor sends money through a Paypal button, but they gave because their Ambassador friend asked them to, how will we know that Ambassador raised that money?

And if we don't know they raised it, we can't thank them. We can't update them on how much they've raised in total. We can't easily keep track of how close all our Ambassadors are to their goals. Or if we do somehow do all this, it will be with lots of emails to a growing number of Ambassadors (remember – we were hoping for hundreds), back and forth, trying to keep track of everything. It would be a nightmare and a full-time job for the project manager, and would almost certainly have led to some cliff-diving, hopefully with a parachute.

Salsa allows for each Ambassador to create their own fundraising page. It tracks who has given, and how much, to each Ambassador, and the total raised is on the page so everyone can see how close they are to the goal. This is good, because it utilizes the momentum principle I talked about earlier with regard to the Matching in May campaign, but just on a smaller scale.

In other words, if an Ambassador has a goal to raise $1000, and everyone going to their page sees they're at $700, that fact - all by itself - will motivate some people to give. And they'll hit and probably exceed their goal.

We had several Ambassadors blow past their original goals, and they reset them at higher levels to keep the momentum going. All this is made possible with a CRM that supports peer-to-peer giving.

Not only that, but anyone who gives online has their contact information entered in the CRM. That means a whole bunch of great stuff can happen, such as thank you emails, newsletter updates, and other follow-up marketing. And with the now less-frazzled project manager smiling again, she might actually have time to make some of those important tasks happen.

Autoresponder Emails

These are so helpful, and so simple a concept, and yet without a CRM, basically impossible. Once you have a donor's contact information, you can send email autoresponders. And you can do this every time someone takes actions you want them to take.

For example, you can set up one autoresponder for their official giving receipt (vital for tax purposes, and expected of any reputable nonprofit).

But you can have an entirely separate autoresponder thank you letter. Why separate them? Because it's better that way! Getting a receipt isn't fun. It's just paperwork. In fact, it's a negative reminder of how much money you just gave away. It almost guarantees some second guessing, wondering if you should have really done that. And if they ask you later for more money, and the only thing you heard from them last time was a tax receipt, you'll be less likely to respond to future requests.

But being thanked - that's when you can reinforce the donor's selfless and transformative decision to give.

Not thanking donors is a cardinal sin in fundraising (of which many are guilty). And waiting too long to thank them doesn't help. Your thank you email needs to be sent quickly if it's going to accomplish its main goal - help the person feel good about what they just did, and direct them to other ways they can take action. And that doesn't mean to give again. Don't ask for more money in your thank you letter. That annoys your donor. They're thinking, "I just gave, and now you want more?"

But you can send them to a blog article with a story of a person your organization has helped. You can send them a special link to a video thank you from a person high up in the nonprofit, or even better, from a person their money will help. You can tell them about volunteer opportunities. You can ask them to share their decision on social media. The thank you email can do wonders.

The absence of one robs you of guaranteed future donations, and weakens the tenuous bond you've just formed with a new donor. You need to nurture and strengthen that bond, just like a new plant that just broke through the soil. Now is the time, in this tender beginning stage, to heap on the water of thanksgiving and appreciation.

A CRM makes this easy and effortless. Here's how it works: Your copywriter (not your project manager; definitely not your founder or CEO) writes one thank you email. That email gets uploaded into the CRM, and set up as an autoresponder anytime someone donates money. The donor receives the email the same day, moments after they give. It works. It's fast. And it allows your project manager to focus on other tasks. And again - this email comes separately from the giving receipt. With a CRM, that's easy.

Event Management
The CRM also allows for event promotion, registrations, and attendance-tracking. That alone is a reason to get one, if you're hoping to hold a live event like we did.

The Absolute Necessity of Investing in Support Systems

If you've never put on a fundraising event and have no experience with it, you may have little sense of the work involved. But if you have worked on one, even as just one volunteer, you quickly learn how much planning and organization goes into it.

Event planning is an industry all its own. For fundraisers, holding an event without a CRM to assist is like running a company without HR or administration. It's a disaster from day one. We'll talk more about lessons we learned from our event in Lesson #7.

But in terms of having a system in place, our event could not have succeeded without a CRM. It puts all the administrative tasks behind the scenes, where they belong.

I could go on for much longer about the value of a CRM. The autoresponders, the data tracking, the flexibility to try new things and to adapt to changes in strategy - the benefits go on and on.

And yes, there is a cost. Our system cost a few thousand dollars. And as I said at the start, the process to get it set up (let alone maintain it - this becomes a primary task of the project manager) is laborious and at times emotionally exhausting.

But we raised $475,000. We simply couldn't have done it without Salsa. If you say a few thousand is too costly an investment, then you are also saying you don't want to raise big money. You simply can't have one without the other.

Lesson 3 Fundraising Takeaway

Your Action Step based on Lesson 3 has two parts:

1) Research nonprofit-specific CRMs and choose the one that best aligns with your goals, tasks, and budget. A few others besides Salsa you can look into include eTapestry, Classy, Donorperfect, and many others.

2) Get someone on your team who can devote the time to manage it, and who has the professionalism and commitment you're going to need. You can't afford to lose this person mid-campaign, especially if it's a one-time campaign like ours.

If you run an ongoing program, this is something you need multiple people to be trained on, and any new hires need to be brought up to speed as part of their onboarding. (And please, don't demand new hires already know your CRM. Find someone who learns well and is responsible and reliable, and train them how to use it. You're costing yourself great people by requiring these specialty demands on new staff before they're hired. If they know it already, consider yourself blessed).

Should you pay someone to manage this, or use a volunteer? Technically, you could do it either way. But, does it matter? Oh, yes. Most certainly. In fact, it matters so much, the answer to this question is Lesson #4.

Lesson 4

Paid Workers Get It Done. Volunteers Support the Paid Workers.

YOU CAN'T DO IT ALL WITH VOLUNTEERS. LET ME SAY THAT AGAIN. YOU CAN'T DO it all with volunteers. No, I'm sorry, you can't.

I can't tell you how many organizations I've worked with or observed from a distance who want more volunteers to do high-skilled development and administrative work. Or work on their website. And this is why so many (especially small) nonprofits never escape feeling stuck in the mire of not having enough resources.

If you don't invest, you won't grow. It's that simple.

If you try to get by with free labor, and avoid paying people to do the tasks that require consistent attention and at least a measure of expertise, <u>you will not save money</u>, and you will be overworked and worn out all the time. You will actually save more money by paying people to do these tasks. How is that possible? Because you'll make more in the long run.

We could not have raised $475,000 without a paid project manager, copywriter, or designer. It just wouldn't have happened. I was there for nine months before we launched our campaign, and stayed through the whole thing past the end point. I saw how the volunteer laborers worked, and I saw how the paid staff (I was the copywriter) worked.

Here's a brief rundown of what each type of worker accomplished:

Paid Workers:

Interviewed the Hetauda House founder

Organized various tasks and initiatives online using Trello

Wrote and sent out regular emails

Wrote content for the website

Coordinated and planned all the event details

Communicated with volunteers to help them make deadlines, including supporting them in various endeavors they were doing, such as the restaurant fundraiser

Supported ambassadors in the events they wanted to do

Created a lot of forms - online and offline, for all sorts of purposes

Ran Facebook promotions for several months

Added captions to online videos

Monitored analytics for website, social media, email, and other giving channels

Tracked all donations (since the paid bookkeeper couldn't keep up)

Worked with Construction for Change on two separate contracts - including in-person meetings and email and phone communication

Researched and wrote grants

Spoke at various public meetings

Sent WPC founder phone numbers of donors to call and thank

Worked with Salsa

Updated the progress of the campaign on the website

Supervised the re-working of the website

Planned team meetings and follow up afterward to keep people on task

Created Powerpoints

Wrote and created graphics for Ambassador packet

Created fliers, brochures, donor cards, and other print materials

Designed T-shirt and executed the sales campaign

Created, edited, and uploaded videos

Kept track of physical materials for use in future events and campaigns

Organized photos in a useful format

Helped people give in ways that worked for them other than our automated channels

Responded to donor needs

Kept the team positive in the face of letdowns and setbacks, of which there were many

Secret Insight: How Paid Work Differs from Volunteer Work

Keep in mind, that is just a partial list, and it's partial in two different ways. If we were to keep thinking about it more, we would remember probably twice this many things the paid staff did.

But it's also a partial list in that, had we been paid more and had more time to execute - we would have done far more. And had this been a permanent nonprofit, we would have burnt out because these are full-time jobs, and we did them in less than 20 hours per week.

The main thing to note here has nothing to do with how hard we worked. That entire list of tasks and accomplishments has one thing - one very crucial thing in common that you must understand:

Continuous attention required.

These aren't tasks you can do on an evening here, a weekend there, a day off now and then, and after you put the kids to bed or finish your homework. These are ongoing, persistent needs and tasks that, if they don't get done, then nothing moves forward and you don't raise the money and your campaign fails. These tasks are the reason you succeed.

A project manager has to MANAGE the project. A copywriter has to produce consistent content to keep the donors and the supporters engaged - especially on a limited-time campaign. A designer has to create a constant flow of graphics to support the writer and the manager. And all this gets done, in part, to facilitate the volunteers doing what they do.

If you think you can put up a crowdfunding page for a big fundraising goal and let it just sit there while you watch donations come in because you mention it now and then on Facebook in between your political rants, bunny pictures, meal photos, and sports trash talking, you will be severely disappointed.

Without paid staff, your volunteers, activists, ambassadors, and other supporters will not know what to do, when to have it done, or how to manage all the details that come up anytime you try to do something that requires planning, organization, and content. They just won't. People need direction. And volunteers don't direct, because they don't have the time it takes to be prepared enough to do so.

If you want truly <u>reliable</u> laborers, who will answer their phone, reply back on email, and respond immediately whenever something comes up, you have to pay them. It's pretty simple, really. Paid workers work.

Volunteer Workers:

Okay, let's take a step back and look at some of the things our wonderful volunteers accomplished.

Created icons for Christmas giving campaign
Created fliers, donor cards, and other print materials
Spoke at events
Planned and executed their own events at theaters, bars, homes, colleges, workplaces
Called and talked to friends and colleagues to ask for support
Created 3-D visual displays for use at events
Showed up to help at events (seeing a theme here? Fundraising events are impossible without volunteers)
Attended planning meetings
Did all the logistics for the restaurant fundraiser
Posted on social media
Set up T-Spring account
Typed emails into Salsa
Looked at grant sites to see if we actually qualify for them
Helped with vision, planning, and working with Construction for Change

Paid Workers Get It Done. Volunteers Support the Paid Workers.

Performed website technical improvements and troubleshooting
Hosted and redesigned website
Babysat so project manager could work longer (yes, really)

As you can see, we had some all-star volunteers. They put in hundreds of hours, collectively. And I've probably missed a few. Their sacrifice, heroism, selflessness, and passion often left us awed and amazed. And some of their work, just like some of ours, produced very little reward for how much time they put in.

It's often a thankless job, which is why YOU as the fundraiser need to thank them - often. And that's a job we probably neglected. We did not thank them enough. But why did this get neglected? Because an effective 'thank you' program, whether to volunteers or to donors, requires a particular ingredient if it's going to be done well. You know what ingredient I'm talking about, right?

Continuous attention from paid staff.

You can't rely on volunteers to run a thank you program for volunteers. Or donors. Yes, your volunteers can *execute* your thank you program. But they will need direction from someone who is paid. Someone who can coordinate the frequent deadlines, who knows what campaigns have been run, who can produce the written content, and who can help the volunteers know what to say, who to call, etc.

So I hope my main point is coming through clearly. This is in no way a criticism of volunteers, and I hope it's not coming across like that. This is an attempt to clarify proper roles. Volunteers do vital work, but that work is supported by paid staff. If you have no paid staff, or not enough paid staff, your campaign will have a ceiling, above which you will never climb. I can't say what our ceiling would have been, because our leadership recognized from the beginning they needed to invest in paid staff. Even though they had very limited funds, they prioritized them where it counted.

The thing you need to understand is that volunteer tasks are isolated. They are discrete. They have start points and end points. Volunteer work should never be ongoing, because you don't want to be in a position of organizational dependence on a volunteer. What if their life circumstances change? *You will be the first thing they give up* on their schedule.

For many nonprofits, social media is an exception to this rule of discreet tasks – which is why, incidentally, organizations that rely on volunteers for social media usually have terrible social media marketing. Social media, even more than email, absolutely depends on a consistent output. Lesson #9 is all about the need for social media expertise.

We had three different social media volunteers at various times, and one paid person. Guess which one, out of the four, posted consistently, on time, and without having to be told? You got it.

Volunteers simply aren't suitable for any tasks that require ongoing attention over months or years.

Volunteers need direction from the people planning and coordinating.

Lesson 4 Fundraising Takeaway

Whether you're planning a limited-time campaign like Hetauda House, or you're part of an established nonprofit with an ongoing mission, you need to work out a clear division of roles.

1) Identify your essential tasks. Assign them to hired staff and freelancers.

There is no end to the needs you can come up with for volunteers to work on. If a volunteer comes in with a particular set of skills, say yes! But understand that any job requiring high-level skills or ongoing attention will never be filled with a volunteer for very long.

I once worked with a nonprofit for about a year on various copywriting tasks including direct mail, print materials, and their website.

In that year, they had two different website volunteers come in. One had design and technical skills, the other had strategic fundraising and planning experience at a much larger nonprofit and wanted to volunteer to help this much smaller one.

Neither one lasted more than two months. Both made promises about all the stuff they would do, and both actually accomplished less than one tenth of it. It wasn't long before they stopped responding to emails and disappeared. And again, the point is not to criticize these people. The point is - they just don't have time for *this kind of work*. It's all-consuming. It is a job, and there's simply no way around it. High-skill positions cannot be done by volunteers because the need for them never ends.

Invest in paid staff to ensure your essential work gets done. And if you don't know what work qualifies as essential work, there's a special opportunity only available at the end of this book that you can use to get help figuring it out. Knowing your essential tasks is one of the first steps to creating a fundraising plan that will succeed. And the same tasks are not essential on all campaigns.

> 2) Create a support system for your existing volunteers that your paid staff will administer.

Our project manager supported dozens of volunteers in all sorts of tasks. Especially when you have volunteers going out and speaking about or promoting your work, you need to make sure they don't misrepresent your mission and values. That means, give them the right support materials, and make sure they have a clear and accurate message.

We created lots of print materials like brochures and response cards, and then we told our volunteers and Ambassadors how to use them. For instance, we wanted contact information for anyone willing to give or sign up for the newsletter. Most volunteers wouldn't think of that, because that's an organizational goal, an internal need.

Do you see how, if the volunteers were just left on their own, this would mean fewer donations? Without this support, they would show up the day of their mini-event, and then wonder if they should collect people's names:

"Oh yeah, what if people want to give now? Do we take checks? What about online giving?"

"Yeah, we should give them the website! Can you make a quick run to FedEx and print off some forms?"

Do you see where this is going? These kinds of frantic, last-minute conversations happen because there's no one directing the ship who could have already anticipated all these needs.

The volunteers won't be angry about this lack of support either. If anything, they'll rave about how exciting the whole thing was: "And then we forgot this, and had to run and get that, and we barely made it back in time, and it was crazy, but it was great!"

But it isn't great.

It costs you real donors. And real connections with future donors. Your paid experts will prevent these disasters from happening.

   3) Thank your volunteers, and don't overwork them.

Our campaign was nonstop. We kept trying new ideas all the time. Volunteers dropped off, and new ones came on. And that's okay. Again - they're working for free. Don't forget that. Often, they are not experts in the tasks they're working on.

But if you find yourself continually calling up the same people and asking them to help on another new task, that's your warning sign that you might be overworking them. They have lives too. If you burn them out, then they'll walk in one day and tell you how much they love working with you, but that they have so much to do and can't give it the time it requires anymore.

The truth is, they can't give the time it requires because they've been doing work that a paid worker should be doing. They've been overworked.

Beware of burning out your best allies.

Follow these three principles, and you guarantee your campaign keeps moving forward, even as volunteers come and go. There's a lot more we could say about volunteers, but this is the primary lesson I learned in the Hetauda campaign.

Lesson 5

Quality Volunteers are Priceless – Do Not Neglect Them

FEW NONPROFITS CAN SUCCEED WITHOUT THE HELP OF COMMITTED VOLUN-teers. For one-time campaigns especially, this is absolutely true. There are simply too many tasks for a handful of paid staff to get done.

We needed volunteers for all sorts of tasks we could not have otherwise done. You just saw a long list of some of those tasks in the last Lesson.

But here's the other thing we learned about volunteers: Not all of them will succeed.

We had an ambitious college student put a huge amount of work into planning an event on her campus. The purpose was to get students in the room, show them the documentary, talk about the project, and try to get some of them involved.

We know college students have no money, so donations weren't the goal. The goal was involvement. At that point in our project (nearing the end), we had very specific needs. We wanted more Ambassadors. A student might not have money, but they have networks they can tap for a couple thousand dollars, if they put the effort in. We hoped for at least a couple of these.

This volunteer student was very confident she could get at least 50 people in the room, maybe more if the news spread beyond her network of friends. Our paid project manager worked with her on all the logistics, and empowered her to plan and run the event. She got a room, got materials to give away, set up the technology to show the video, and all the rest. She also marketed it – to her friends, their friends, her dorm, and every other group she was part of.

And this is when a hard lesson got learned by a disappointed volunteer. It's the first lesson in this book. Not everything you do will work, even when you're sure it will.

She didn't get 50 people. She got 8.

What a letdown. She was pretty crushed. And of those 8, none signed up to be Ambassadors. None donated.

One side lesson – being an Ambassador, even though it doesn't cost you money, still takes time. And these days, most people would rather spend two hours on social media than do something useful. People do have time – don't let anyone tell you otherwise (including yourself). Everyone has time. It's just in how they choose to use it. I don't have time to write books. And yet, here you are.

This volunteer's event did get two people who said they'd volunteer, and a few who signed up for the newsletter. But what happened when we followed up with the two who said they'd volunteer? No response. We sent them multiple emails, and never got a single response. And no one forced them to sign up, so there's no reason they would have given a fake email. If you don't want to volunteer, then don't sign up, right?

For whatever reason, they just didn't really want to help.

And no one says they have to. The point is, you will get way more "volunteers" than you'll ever actually meet in person. In my experience, over half the people who volunteer won't take a single action, and you'll never hear from them again. They won't respond to emails or phone calls. My hunch is, they volunteer probably because they don't understand what it means to *commit* to something, and something you said produced an emotional response. But that emotional response didn't translate into real interest or action.

Whatever the reason, this happens, and you need to expect it.

Now, the flip side of this is the even more important part. When you do find good volunteers - people who actually show up - you need to nurture and empower them. Some of this got covered in the last Lesson, but it bears a little extra attention here.

First, what is a quality volunteer? Here's a good checklist. If you see a majority of these traits in someone you aren't paying, you know you have someone who deeply cares about your mission. They own it, and you don't have to convince them to show up. You just have to ask, and if they have the ability to do so, they'll say yes.

Traits of All-Star Volunteers

- √ Shows up
- √ Offers ideas you hadn't thought of
- √ Does the legwork necessary to complete a task, without having to be told (initiative)
- √ Asks you what else they can do
- √ Tells other people about your work, and brings more volunteers to you (your 'evangelist')
- √ Suffers for you - even to the point of investing their own money in a task and not asking for reimbursement
- √ Arrives on time to time-sensitive situations, like events
- √ Has a good attitude

Let's be clear – no one owes you any of this. That's what makes this person a QUALITY volunteer. They just are this way. Your only possible response is to gush with gratitude and thankfulness.

So, the student who put on the failed event was a quality volunteer. It doesn't matter that her event didn't succeed. The fact she went the extra mile, many times over, to make it happen, proved to us she cared about our success. How we respond to her failed event is very, very important. Don't give her the silent treatment, and don't criticize.

As experienced fundraisers, we should know not everything works, even when it's planned well like this one was. But holding on to the volunteer and keeping her motivated and feeling like she still has more to contribute – that's the outcome you want.

We had another volunteer, one I already mentioned, who went out on her own to Nepali and Indian restaurants to ask the owners if we could do a joint fundraiser with them. Our proposal was that they could give us a portion of the proceeds from their food sales for a day.

She got two takers, and both of these events raised several hundred dollars for relatively little effort on our part. But it wasn't little effort on her part. She spent hours driving to them, talking in person, talking on the phone, working out the details, and doing this for several restaurants, some of which didn't pan out.

This volunteer also transcribed newsletters into Salsa and formatted them, did printing for us, and brought a sense of optimism at one of the lowest points of the campaign.

Lesson 5 Fundraising Takeaway

For your top volunteers, here's a respectful and empowering action plan for how to work with them so they keep helping you for years, don't burnout, and feel valued and appreciated.

> √ Give them work they can manage within their available time. Do NOT overwork them.

Quality Volunteers are Priceless – Do Not Neglect Them

- √ Give them work within their skillset. Don't ask a shy high school student to cold call business owners. And don't ask a 74-year old to update your website (in most cases).
- √ Ask them if what you're having them do is too much. You don't want them overwhelmed.
- √ Don't assume you're overworking them - ask! A few of our volunteers were unemployed for several months. They had lots of time, and didn't mind giving it to us.
- √ Prioritize their mental and emotional health, even over your mission. Make sure they're doing well. If something goes badly, take time to talk it through and encourage them. Your mission will always be there. But a superstar volunteer? Not easy to replace.
- √ Don't expect them to donate. They probably will if they can, but just like everyone else, they don't have to. They are donating their time, sweat, and expertise. That's as valuable as money, if not more.
- √ Prioritize their projects over your own. We had another volunteer who spent massive amounts of time planning her own little fundraising event. She tried to corral a bunch of local churches to show up. Almost no one did, in spite of all her tireless effort. It did bring in some funds, but nothing near what the effort merited. And we supported her the whole way with strategies, materials, and suggestions. We invested in her success, and then we shared in her disappointment. She never felt alone.
- √ Thank them, as often as possible. Do it in writing. Do it over the phone. Do it in person. Doing it by text is worthless, because texting is so thoughtless and trite that it barely has any meaning.
- √ These people already know they aren't doing this for money. But if you take their work for granted, they will feel undervalued and underappreciated. And that's a disaster, because when they quit (which they will), and someone asks them why, what do you think they'll say?
- √ Put them in charge. If there's something that requires a larger amount of help, put the people in charge who have proven themselves. Even if someone else shows up at the last minute who may have more

expertise. That person isn't invested in your mission yet, and skills without empathy comes across as insincere.

- √ Recognize their work, publicly. If you have an event, call out your top volunteers by name. Put their pictures in your newsletter. Let them speak by giving a welcome or sharing why they like to work for you. Give them an actual award, or thank them with a gift certificate or something related to your work. Let them record videos for training or other purposes. In other words, let them be the faces of your organization. They are walking testimonials. Employees can't give testimonials. They work for you. But volunteers can, and your all-star ones should be front and center (with their consent, of course. Some people don't want public recognition).

- √ Invite them to your celebrations and important meetings. Involve them as much as they want to be involved. The more they intertwine with your work, and the more they understand everything you do, the better they can explain and represent you with passion and positivity to people in their lives.

The bottom line is - these people are as valuable as your paid workers, and yet they aren't being paid. That makes them even higher than your paid staff in terms of how you should relate to them. They are honorable, so honor them.

Especially for ongoing missions and causes, this is absolutely vital.

Lesson 6

Do not Leave Big Decisions to People without Expertise

WHY DO PEOPLE GIVE AWAY THEIR MONEY?

Have you ever stopped to ponder that? If you call yourself a fundraiser, I sure hope you have! It is your awareness to even ask this question that separates you from anyone else - even people you work with - and makes you a person who should have decision-making power over fundraising plans and implementation.

I ask this to expose a deeper issue - the appalling lack of expertise that gets entrusted with decisions of expansive consequence. You simply cannot afford to leave the biggest decisions about your fundraising to people who have little experience or expertise.

But what is expertise? How can you tell if someone, including yourself, has knowledge, experience, and understanding that represents more than just the opinions of a casual observer or the whims of someone who "feels" like a certain course of action is a good idea?

Identifying and Gaining Fundraising Expertise

To begin, let's be clear what expertise *doesn't* mean. If you ever hear any of these phrases, they tell you nothing about this person's actual expertise in fundraising:

"I've worked on lots of fundraising campaigns."
"I have a degree in nonprofit organizational development."
"I've been a volunteer for this organization for a while."
"I'm on the board."
"I'm the founder."
"I care so much about this issue."
"I've been working here a long time."
"I give to a lot of causes."

An important note - if you run into any of these kinds of people, you should be nice to them, because they sound like superb assets for your organization. People who say these things can be great volunteers, board members, champions for your cause, ambassadors, donors, employees, and much more. These people can all help you.

But they might not be fundraisers. They might be, but these kinds of statements don't help you to know.

So how can you identify fundraising expertise? Surprisingly, you can be an expert without having ever raised a single penny. How? By *studying* fundraising.

For me, I get mail from a lot of nonprofits, and I read it. I also attend fundraising events and auctions, and even participate in them. I look at how they present their case. How do they begin their letters and emails? How do they tell their story? What do they do at events? Who speaks, and how does the audience seem to react?

I also think about the ones I have given money to, and I ask myself what it was that helped convince me to give. And, I think about why I don't give, or why I limit my giving to certain amounts. Why do I give recurring gifts here, but only one-time gifts there?

So, some expertise comes from simple observation, learning from what works (and what doesn't work), and just reflecting on it. Reflection is a lost art. If your fundraising team never reflects on their methods, and just keeps doing "what we do every year," that's a bad sign.

Now, if it's working, that's great. But what else can you do? What can you do to make it better? Is there anything you could test it against? Reflect on it, and see what you come up with.

Expertise also comes from learning from other experts. Read fundraising blogs and newsletters. A lot. Learn what others are doing, and what data they have to show what works well. Reading this book is a great way to build your expertise.

And of course, expertise also comes from actually doing fundraising. The important thing is – it can come from failure and as well as success. Why? Because **expertise means you learned something**, and you learn from failure as much as you learn from success. I once had a guy denounce my entire business because of a single click-through rate in a single Adwords campaign and no other contextual information. As if anyone *always* scores high CTRs on Adwords.

In this Hetauda campaign, as you read earlier, many of our ideas failed. Fell flat as a pancake. We also succeeded in some. But we *learned* from all of it, and we now have even more expertise than we had when we started.

To recap – expertise comes from doing fundraising, learning from your successes and failures by reflecting on it, studying what others have done and are doing, and learning from other experts. It does not come from earning a college degree. Sorry. Expertise only happens in the real world.

Why Expertise Must Be Given Decision-Making Authority

This is a huge issue, and it can be hard to fight for. Many charities have people on their team who are passionate, devoted, outgoing, strong-willed, positive, charismatic, and many other good traits, but who have no actual fundraising expertise.

And it's very easy to be drawn to those people. Ever been in a room like that? There's all kinds of discussion going on. It's a brainstorming-fest. Healthy dialogue.

Some good respectful arguments here and there. Maybe some not-so-respectful ones too.

But then that one person who everyone kind of likes gets up and says what they think. The room gets much quieter than it was when *you* were talking. Heads start nodding even before the person finishes speaking. It just seems so important, what they're saying. A bit more profound. Look how thoughtful they sound. And we all know how much this person cares about this, how long they've been working "on the ground" and "in the field."

And before you know it, that's the last word. Suddenly you're implementing their ideas, even though that quiet person who spoke up earlier had what you thought was a far better idea that has now been forgotten.

You have to be careful who gets final authority, and make it clear before you end up in discussions like that.

Let's now turn and look at some practical ways this can play out in your organization.

What Do We Do?

Here's a big area of disagreement: *How much information should you give potential donors?*

Should you tell them the history of your organization and its founding? How about how your program operates, and what you do? Should you talk about your staff and what they do? Your volunteers? Should you say anything about your previous event when marketing the next one? Should you give numbers – how much you've raised, how many people you've helped, how much you spend on 'program' verses administration? What about the real world issues related to your mission? Should we tell people how disastrous the world is because of this injustice or the problem we're trying to solve?

These are BIG questions.

If you asked your staff about each of these, you'd find a wide range of opinions. About all of it. So that begs the question: What do we do?

And more importantly, who gets to decide?

Do you see why expertise is so important here? Some of those questions don't have one answer, necessarily. But some of them do. Sometimes, the answer depends on the context. Are you talking about a fundraising letter? An email? A web page? An event presenter? A brochure? Who's going to see this? What is the purpose of the thing they'll be seeing?

What does expertise look like in this situation?

An expert considers four components, at a minimum:

1) The audience – who is going to see this, and why them?
2) The message – what message do we want this audience to hear? And what message do they want to hear? Are these the same thing? If not, what do we cut?
3) The media – how can we best communicate this message in print, online, on TV, at a live event?
4) The call to action – what do we want the audience to do after they hear the message?

The first item – the audience – is listed first for a reason. The audience is the most important consideration in any fundraising decision. For example:

The Baker, the Runner, and the Unclear Website

Let's say your audience is online, and you've run a Facebook ad telling viewers to click a link and sign up to be part of a fundraising event. Maybe a 5k run or a bake sale. So they click an ad which asks them to be part of this event.

Let's stop here and ask an important question: What kind of person clicks on that link?

If I like to bake, and I see an ad about raising money with a bake sale, *what do I want to see* when I get to the website?

If I like to run, and I see an ad about raising money by running a 5k, *what do I want to see* when I get to the website?

Do I want to learn how to sign up for the bake sale or the 5k? Or do I want to read about the history of your great organization and how your program has saved hundreds of lives this year alone, all because of your tireless staff, devoted volunteers, and passionate advocates?

I, as the baker or the runner, want to sign up. That's my number one goal. At this point in my decision-making, I don't care about the rest of that. I like to bake, and I like to run, and I like the idea of helping some cause by doing what I love. If I can't figure out how to sign up for the event, why would I care about your organization? This is about clarity of purpose and website usability.

So, if signing up is really easy and clear, and I go ahead and do so, then later, I might, maybe, depending on my personality, be interested in some of that other stuff. Maybe.

But it does not belong on THAT webpage. If your ad asks for people to sign up, then the page they land on should be about *signing up*. Not your wonderfulness.

What's the point of this example? The point is, if you have someone on your team telling you to put all that other stuff on the page, because "how else will they know what we do?", that person is <u>wrong</u>, and you need to find a respectful way to tell them so. They are not a fundraising or marketing expert.

This matters, a lot! If you let that person have their way, the lost participants and funds that you'll miss out on will be costly. This is real money. These are real volunteers. This is real momentum. And you'll miss out on a lot of it if you listen to the wrong person.

<u>Passion does not equal expertise.</u>

How A Fundraising Expert Thinks About…

Now, let's look at a few more areas of fundraising where expertise is vital.

1) Event planning

For Hetauda House, we mismanaged our expertise in planning our event, which I'll talk more about in the next chapter. We gave a little too much decision-making power to the event planners. Now, they are great event planners, but they are not fundraisers. And our event was a decent success, so everyone was happy.

But when you're talking about details like what will be on the tables, how people will be greeted, what will be on the screen during the dinner, how your silent auction will be conducted, how the room will be laid out, how to create a schedule that will produce maximum emotional response – these are details that a generic event planner may not have thought about from a fundraising perspective. So, if they're in charge of planning the event, very important things that should happen, won't, because the people in charge simply didn't know.

We realized too late that we had given our event planners a little too much autonomy. So, we had to circle back around and address some of the important items that had been left out. Needless to say, this meant a very frantic couple weeks before the event.

2) Time Mapping

As in, when should you send out emails and direct mail? How often? If you're having an event, when should it be? How long before your event should you start promoting it?

I once volunteered for a tiny nonprofit that wanted to put on an event. Their first choice of a date didn't work out, so they delayed it for a while, which was a smart move. But then, I kept asking when the new date was. When I finally got the new date, it was only a month away!

Let's be clear – one month is nowhere near enough time to market and promote an event. If, that is, you want more than a handful of people to show up. In that instance, they got 20. Not nearly enough.

Expertise understands how to plan ahead and keep consistent messaging going out across multiple channels. Timing is everything. When we planned our 50k

Matching in May campaign and made $100,000 in one month, we started talking about it weeks beforehand. We planned the email campaign, the graphics, the backend support, and the other key elements that made the timing zing.

We capitalized on the momentum of the campaign at that time, but we succeeded because we had expertise about timing.

3) Trends and fads

Ever have anyone come in your office and excitedly tell you about a new app that will help your fundraising? Or a new web tool? As well-known marketing expert Dan Kennedy would say, "Beware of bright shiny objects." If you ever saw "A Bug's Life," then you'll know this reference: Stay away from the light!

They may be pretty, but most gimmicks and doodads are just that – toys, fads, and trends that will pass away before you even figure out what they do.

Expertise doesn't get swayed off course by trends and fads. It knows what works, and knows how to incorporate new tools into what works, if and when appropriate. Expertise does not abandon proven strategies in favor of unproven ones.

The fad that nearly crippled our campaign was the original website that was in place when I arrived. You'll see why it was so crippling in Lesson #11.

4) Doing it in the right order

Here's a specific area where lots of nonprofits (and businesses) do things in the wrong order: They let their web designer design the website without oversight from a fundraising expert.

In general, it is very unwise to set up your website as a first step. You need a lot of other things worked out before then. Like, your message. And those things need to be worked on by someone with expertise.

We made this mistake. We had a web design firm create our website well before any actual fundraising campaign was planned. It was… not a good website. At all. And it cost thousands of dollars to build.

Expertise would have saved us a lot of money (or spent it more wisely) had we done things in the right order.

5) Relying too much on volunteers

We've covered this in the last two Lessons, but it bears repeating here because volunteers are often your most passionate, committed, and inspiring supporters and contributors. So, people naturally listen to them over the boring guy behind the computer.

But, the boring guy might just be smarter when it comes to fundraising. Love your volunteers, but unless they have expertise, take their fundraising advice politely, and filter it through someone with expertise.

We had a lot of cooks in the kitchen over the course of the Hetauda House campaign. I sat in meetings and watched a lot of ideas go around. Some were good. Not all of the good ones came from experts. What does that mean? It means you don't have to be an expert to have good ideas. But expertise is the only way to spot the bad ones.

Why are volunteers not usually good sources of fundraising advice? Because volunteers know your mission and organization even better than you do in some cases. But donors? Especially new donors? They come from a *completely different* perspective. **A typical volunteer will assume other people care about your work**, just like they do. But other people might not care.

I saw this error play out once in a Christian organization that works with human trafficking (yes, I care about this issue…). They brought on a new communications volunteer, and she started sending out these emails that used very strong religious language – of a sort that would make even other Christians feel uncomfortable.

Why was she doing this? Because it's how *she* experienced the work they're doing. And that's fine for her. But it's not how all their supporters perceive it. And it was awkward, uncomfortable (and poorly written, sadly). This kind of miscommunication drives away support more than it strengthens it. Yes, you need to be honest about your mission, but you also need to communicate it in such a way that your supporters can go with you.

Most volunteers without fundraising expertise will struggle with this concept. (And this is another example of why volunteers should not be writing any communication with donors, except perhaps scripted thank you letters. Donor communication is best done by paid experts).

6) Manage your time

Some good ideas simply can't be accomplished depending on your resources. Expertise understands how to work within your constraints and use resources wisely.

It will stop you from investing hundreds of man-hours on projects that are unlikely to produce more than a few hundred dollars in donations. A disturbingly high number of events fall into this trap. If someone proposes an event, make sure you talk to an expert to work out the logistics that would be required to actually make it happen, and see if you have the people, the time, the money, and the tools to do it.

Expertise says 'no' when other people say 'yes.'

7) How are you going to get your message out?

There are lots of ways to get your message out: Email, live events, webinars, Facebook, Google, peer-to-peer, traditional media, direct mail, and more. All these require targeted messaging and logistical support. All require an upfront strategy. And how you decide which ones to use depends on the audience (or audiences) you're targeting.

For instance, many people say direct mail is dead. Those people aren't experts. Now, we didn't do any direct mail with Hetauda House because direct mail works best if you can do it continually, and our campaign was limited – our original goal was to raise all the funds in four months.

A one-time direct mail campaign is tough to do if you want a big return for your investment, which is higher up front. But an ongoing direct mail campaign, done well, has a high probability of bringing in consistently positive returns. A lot of that has to do with audience – the people who actually read their mail are also the people who give way more to charity. (If you're not sure who those people are, ask your grandmother).

But that's the point here. Expertise considers the best way to get your message out. A lot of charities resist direct mail because of the costs. If you have an established nonprofit and you aren't doing direct mail, you're probably missing out on a source of funds.

Expertise says 'yes' when other people say 'no.'

When we got our breakthrough $50,000 gift in April, as I pointed out earlier, we had to face the question of how to share this with supporters. Some suggested doing a Facebook or Twitter blast. But by this time, we had learned that some announcements needed to be managed and planned more carefully. Our final decision to wait, and to release that news as part of the '50k Matching in May' idea, proved to be the decisive moment of the entire campaign.

There are plenty of misconceptions about email, Facebook, webinars, eBooks, live events, and all the other ways to get your message out. Just because something worked for someone else doesn't mean it will work for you. Your audience, and the best media to reach them, might be different.

Where you invest your fundraising dollars matters. You need to do more than read a couple blogs and think you've found the answer.

What Do We Say?

I've talked a lot here about your 'message.' But what is your message? Whatever the form of media, what do you say to engage your current donors and attract new ones?

Whole books could be written on this subject, so it's impossible to do it justice here. But here's the most important thing you need to know about messaging: **People give because of words**.

Remember the question I asked at the start of this chapter (and the book)? Why do people give away their money? Understanding the answer is why you need an expert, because the answer to that affects everything you say, write, photograph, or record.

Here's a couple examples that will make this point clear:

1) TV fundraising commercials

You've seen them. The sad puppy behind the bars. The hungry children. The music. Do these commercials really work? The fact they keep doing them year after year tells me they do. This is direct response fundraising. They know how many people give based on these ads. They wouldn't keep doing them if people weren't giving.

But think about seeing one of those ads without sound, and if there were no words on the screen. Even the most moving and tragic pictures don't have the same effect without words - either written or from a voice artist. Words help us contextualize what we're seeing, and motivate us to action. Otherwise they're just sad pictures. It's the words that provoke a response.

Why am I making this point? Because I see it done wrong over and over and over again, especially online. Our original site had almost no words on it. It was assumptive, which violates the Lesson 0 axiom you saw at the beginning of this book. No words means no message. No message means no one knows what to do or has a reason to do it.

Take a lesson from TV fundraising ads. Whether you like that style or not, there is a lot to learn from it, because it works (and, they know their audience).

2) Email

Some emails have no pictures. Some have way too many. Most have one or two. And pictures are powerful. I'm in no way saying you shouldn't use pictures.

But think about an email that has only a picture and no message to go with it. Would anyone give? Why would they? There's nothing to grab hold of. On the other hand, can an email with only words motivate people to give? It sure can.

The point is – pictures are not the message. Pictures *support* the message. The message takes what people may see in a photo, graphic, or video, and tells them how to feel about it, and what to do about it.

In email especially, your first message is your subject line. If you don't get people past that, the most amazing and moving pictures in the world, sitting inside an unopened email, mean nothing. So you need a message, and you need to express it in a way that people react to. You need to get their attention, and focus it on one idea.

I've seen email subject lines that are so long they don't fit in the space allotted. And I don't mean on a smartphone, which has even less space. I mean on a desktop. And so confusing too. Filled with numbers, dates, and titles. Sloppy beyond belief.

In the same way, broad, vague, organization-focused subject lines are guaranteed to get lower open rates. I sent out an end-of-year email series once. It had four emails total, the last one coming on December 31st. But #3, the one right before it, had a person's name in the subject line, a woman who had been helped by this particular nonprofit. It was "her story." That email beat our average open rates by five percentage points. If you have 50,000 people on your email list, how many people is 5%? 2500.

The right message means thousands more people get engaged with your mission.

   3) Websites

Again, you could write a whole book about nonprofit websites. But allow me to tell you my biggest complaint with almost every nonprofit site I visit (and I visit a lot of them).

What we see on the home page – the first page most of your visitors will see – is a massive image that takes up the entire screen, with a tiny message in the middle of it. All the rest of the screen is just a picture. And that message is focused on only one idea, often not the reason I personally came to the site.

This is failed web marketing. It's a failure of message, market, and media - all three of the most important parts of fundraising. Why? Because it doesn't consider the needs of your visitors. Why does someone visit a nonprofit's website? Think about all the possible reasons:

Curiosity - heard about it somewhere

Referral - a friend told them to check it out

Confirmation - they saw an ad or something, and want to see if it's for real

Missional alignment - they care about the same issue as you, and want to see if they can work with you

Donation - they want to give

Engagement - they want to join your email list and start learning more about you

Volunteering - they want to get involved and make a direct impact

We could probably come up with 20 more. Do you see why the single sentence on a huge screen with a meaningless picture is a failure? It disregards 95% of the reasons people might visit your site. It presumes there's only one message for everyone, and one way to get involved.

All the other messaging is buried in hard to find menus and in sparse graphics with hardly any words. I have to already know a lot about this organization to interact with what I see on most nonprofit home pages.

Every home page and every other page on your site needs a message. People online are looking for quick engagement, simplicity, and most of all - **clarity**. Pictures aren't clear by themselves. Those huge images filling up almost every nonprofit's home page? They're accomplishing very little except to annoy me as I scroll through them so I can do what I really came to do.

This is one example of what I mean by putting design before message. A designer, not a fundraiser, had too much authority in the creation of a site like that.

Your home page needs messaging that speaks to as many people as possible. And take note - this doesn't mean huge menus with 15 dropdown menus each (though, those were a lot easier to navigate...just saying). Yes, we have to be aware of the restrictions forced upon usability because of the proliferation of mobile devices.

But where you put your menus. The words you use to label them. How easily a person can get through a page and be engaged by your message and mission. This matters.

Few people will give just because of one visit to your website. It's only one part of your overall fundraising strategy. But you need to take full advantage of what a website can do. Otherwise you're turning away people who might have become volunteers, supporters, and donors.

At Hetauda, when we rewrote the site after the first version was found to be inadequate, we wrote it with all this in mind. We made it possible to learn more about what the Hetauda House will do. We told them where their money would go, what the new building would be like, how it would change lives and transform a community. We showed pictures of the kids. The food that gets prepared for them. The schools they get sent to because of generous donations from their supporters.

Why did we do all this? Why didn't we just show one video, ask for money, ask people to become ambassadors, and call it good?

Because we needed to raise $500,000 in less than a year with only a handful of volunteers and a few partially paid staff! That means we need more than just donors. We need allies. Champions. Ambassadors who will sacrifice their own time and money to help. We need people to suffer, of their own free will, for our cause.

You don't win a champion ally with one sentence.

Lesson 6 Fundraising Takeaway

How do you recognize expertise? And especially if you have a low budget, how do you afford it? Let's take these one at a time.

Recognize Expertise – Ask the Right Questions

Here's a set of questions to ask someone who says they can help you raise more money. You could call this the Quack Test of fundraising, to sift out the imposters.

1) Why do you think people give their money away, and can you give an example?

You're not looking for a specific answer here. You're looking for their thought process. Their reflective skills. Their values, perhaps. They will reveal their experience and knowledge about fundraising from this question, way more than if you asked the dry, boring, obvious question of "what is your experience?" Don't ask that. Use this question, and you will draw it out.

2) What can we do to encourage more people to give, and to give larger amounts?

Here you're looking for specifics. Not one specific answer, but again, they should have a lot of ideas spew out. This is the kind of question an expert loves, because they can just talk about all kinds of things. You'll be able to tell if they can help you. As a bonus, their passion might show itself too – usually a good sign.

3) Describe one of the hardest fundraising situations you've been a part of. (Follow-up with this, if they don't offer it themselves: What did you learn from it?)

Remember – expertise doesn't mean you win every time. <u>If they haven't failed before, they are not an expert</u>. If they can't point to a failure, but claim lots of fundraising experience, what this likely means is they were part of a team, but weren't in charge of any big decisions. So, this person might be helpful, but they are not someone to regard as an expert.

Listen to an expert talk about one of their failures and what they learned, and you'll again see that crucial element you must have in fundraising: reflection.

>4) What do you consider your greatest area of fundraising expertise?

This is a big one, because there are many possible answers. Some people excel at building connections with businesses or major donors, for example. Others might do well with online fundraising strategies, live events, or be good on the phone. You might also find someone who writes great content, or someone who works best behind the scenes, setting up systems that make donating easier and the messaging able to reach more people. You might find a person who just knows all the resources you need to raise funds and will connect you with them and help you set them up. This person might never write a word of content or talk to a single supporter, but they have expertise that will grow your nonprofit in big ways.

What you're not looking for is, "I have a degree in" something. I don't want to disparage college degrees too much. But they are way overrated in this particular area. For certain skillsets, they matter a lot. But take Hetauda House for example. No one on our team has any degrees related to fundraising. That's not where our success came from. So if you want to make college degrees in specific fields a litmus test for finding fundraising expertise, you are free to do so. But you're barking up the wrong tree while better talent sits on the grass right next to you.

This question again lets them fill in the blanks for you, and tells you their strengths. No one is good at everything. You want to know this person's greatest value, and if that's what you need most at this moment.

>5) If a recurring donor stops giving, how would you know, and what would you do?

Here, you're looking for one of two things. Either they're baffled by the question and have no idea how you'd know someone stopped giving, and kind of fumble through a strategy as if it's the first time they've thought of this. Or, they know this is a very important part of fundraising, and will talk about the importance of personal follow-up, thanking donors, finding out if they just changed their credit card or bank account, and things of that nature.

Take those five questions, adapt them as needed and maybe add a few more, and you'll easily spot someone who can help you.

Afford Expertise – Enlarge the Pool

Look, it's hard to find expertise. I've interacted with dozens of nonprofits. Almost none of them – especially the small ones – had anyone with real fundraising expertise. And some of the bigger nonprofits, if they do have expertise, it sure doesn't show because their websites are terrible.

So your struggle is not unique. But this is one reason I often rant about putting too much trust in college degrees. If your first thought when looking for help is to assume they need a degree "in our field," you've already shrunk the size of the talent pool.

Real fundraising expertise doesn't come from the classroom. I personally have zero classroom experience with fundraising. An absolute zero. Yet here I am, producing content, driving strategies, and seeing organizations who work with me growing. How did I manage this? Well, read this chapter again. No big secret. Just persistence, hard work, and a willingness to sacrifice in order to learn.

And that's the first key to affording expertise: Finding someone who is willing to work at rates you can afford. It's likely you won't be able to hire them full-time. But you don't need that if you're smaller, and who wants the HR headaches? You need an advisor, a consultant, an occasional outside word of guidance, and hopefully, some help implementing too.

Why would someone be willing to work at "rates you can afford?" They might be younger and want experience, and be willing to do so. There are other possible reasons. But I listed the best one earlier because it's also a reason people might visit your website – missional alignment.

If you find someone who cares passionately about your cause who is also an expert, they are likely to be willing to work within your budget, even if it's less than their expertise warrants.

Finally, just do whatever it takes to make it work. If you can only afford $200 a month, or $1500 as a one-time investment with occasional follow-ups, then get whatever you can get for those amounts.

Even for just $100 a month, a good fundraising consultant will give you an hour, maybe two or three hours, of their time. That time can multiply your fundraising efforts by leaps and bounds, and you'll be able to afford more later, after what they're doing for you starts to take effect.

To quickly review, if you want to afford expertise, here are the four steps:

1) Find someone willing to work within your budget
2) Find an ally for your cause who wants you to succeed because they share your passion
3) Do what it takes to make an agreement they are comfortable with, and milk them for whatever they're willing to give.
4) Increase your partnership with them as you begin to grow

Just remember, as we talked about in Lesson #3, you'll often have to invest more upfront, and will lose money for a time, before things swing back the other direction. There are lots of reasons for this, but the main one is that in most cases, so many things aren't being done right, and getting the fundamentals fixed has to happen before growth strategies can even be considered.

For Hetauda House, that meant re-writing their entire website and investing in Salsa Labs. That was an upfront investment, which they made before even launching the official campaign. But when the campaign did finally launch, we had the foundation laid so we could focus purely on fundraising.

The extra few thousand dollars they spent up front resulted in $475,000 by that time next year.

Was it worth it?

Lesson 7

Producing a Successful Event is a Lot Harder than It Looks

THERE'S NOTHING ELSE QUITE LIKE IT IN FUNDRAISING.

Yes, you need recurring donors, volunteers, one-time email campaigns, and other ways of raising revenue. But there's nothing like a successful fundraising auction. An auction, even for a small nonprofit, can jolt your coffers with tens or hundreds of thousands of new revenue in a single day. If you scale it up a bit, you can bring in millions.

This is an important chapter. Much of this book is devoted to general fundraising campaigns and the underlying processes that power them to success.

But live events are a discreet, singular entity. And just like the benefits of live events are unique, so is the work required to plan, market, and execute them. Putting on an event is not something to be undertaken lightly. It will take many hours from many people to make it happen – if, that is, you want more than 20 people to show up.

Fundraising events still have to utilize fundraising and marketing principles, but they also require another set of skills. Many of the decisions you're faced with when putting on an event have little in common with those you deal with in the rest of your fundraising.

As you're about to discover, event fundraising requires more than just a good story. It requires lots of logistics. You aren't just showing a TV commercial and slapping up a phone number asking for money. You are coordinating a whole lot of moving parts, and this coordination begins long before the event, and ends after it's over.

Before I get into the details here, let me start by saying this: There are many types of live events and ways to get your supporters participating interactively. A formal fundraising event or auction like the one we did is not the only way to raise money live. However, in terms of dollar amounts raised in a single day, auctions have the highest ceiling.

But, there is more value to doing an event besides just the donations you get from it. If you do a run/walk event, or a baking contest, or a tree-planting trek, you might only raise a few thousand dollars (or a few hundred). But you might also meet dozens of new enthusiastic contacts you can keep reaching out to, which increases the value of that one event long after the day is over.

For Hetauda House, we decided to do a one-time fundraising event, because we knew this would be the simplest way to raise the maximum amount of funds. We also wanted to use it to kick off the whole campaign, get people energized and motivated, and produce a sense of celebration.

We wanted momentum. And getting 150 people all in one room is a great way to do that. Before we get to the lessons learned, here's a quick rundown of what we did.

Hetauda Heirs of Hope Event

7pm
On a Saturday night, the event began with Nepali appetizers and a silent auction. This went on for half an hour while people got to browse the auction and

make their bids. Some items included photos and artwork from Nepal. Others were donated by people and businesses in our network. During this time, people could also buy raffle tickets.

7:30

Our lead campaign promotor, Perry Burkholder, got up to do a brief welcome, and then introduced the performers coming up next – a dance and spoken word presentation. This was a great way to begin the event. It was impressive enough just from an artistic standpoint, but it also ignited lots of emotion by expressing the pain and brokenness that girls and women caught up in human trafficking live with on a daily basis.

The audience loved it.

7:45

The project manager got up and drew the first raffle ticket. Most events often save all the raffle drawings until the end. But if you have more than one prize, why not mix things up and give people a sense that they have multiple chances to win? It's kind of like the Oscars. They don't save all the big awards for the end. They do Best Supporting Actor and Actress early on so you feel like you got something you wanted without having to sit through the entire five hours.

7:50

We then aired the 20 minute documentary, which was filmed in Nepal. The filmmaker was in the audience, and he gave a brief introduction to his work. This also was a great idea, because the audience could see this film was made by someone with a deep connection to the human trafficking survivors and their suffering. Hearing the filmmaker talk openly and vulnerably about how his experience affected him drew everyone into the story that much more.

8:20

Lila Ghising, the Nepalese founder of the Women's Protection Center in Nepal and its US arm (Friends of WPC Nepal), got up to speak next. Having the founder tell her own story, and express the vision for what we're doing and why, helps anyone in the audience who doesn't know anything about Hetauda understand the impact they can have.

This is important, because it's surprising how many people come to events knowing nothing about the organization putting it on. Someone invited them, maybe even at the last minute, and they decided to come for one reason or another.

But you cannot assume everyone at your event already buys into your mission and vision, or even knows much about you at all. You might be thinking, "Well of course we can't assume that." But I've been to events - bigger ones than ours - where they made this exact mistake.

A live event is your best opportunity to "sell" your cause to people who don't know about it, and to 're-sell' it to ones who do but who might have lost some of the emotional fire and passion that got them involved at first. This is when you re-energize your core supporters and also inspire new ones. Don't throw this chance away by assuming everyone there already knows and cares about your work.

8:30
Perry got up again to deliver the final call to action and appeal. He talked about why the Hetauda House needed to be built, especially in light of the earthquakes that devastated the nation of Nepal earlier that year, including the too-small rented safe home the Women's Protection Center was using at the time.

Perry gave a two-step call to action.

The first step: Give tonight to help build a safe home for women and kids. He also revealed that we got a matching grant from an anonymous foundation that would match the first $50,000 given in the campaign, including at this event.

The second step: Become a Hetauda Ambassador. He talked about the Ambassador program, our peer-to-peer fundraising plan to get our supporters to reach out to their own contacts and multiply donations. As I mentioned in an earlier chapter, this was a central part of our initial strategy.

To incentivize people to sign up, he told them the first 50 people to sign up would get a free Hetauda House T-shirt.

8:45
With that, the audience got some time to give, which they could do in a number of ways: Put their gifts in envelopes that were already on the tables (cash, checks, or a card filled out with their credit card data), or give by credit card on the website afterward.

Then, the silent auction closed and the winning bidders were announced. The final raffle ticket was drawn, and the event was concluded.

The Final Tally – Was It Worth It?

In all – including ticket sales to attend the event, the raffle, the silent auction, and the donations – this relatively small event produced over $22,000. With costs of just around $5000, we were thrilled with such a great start to our campaign. In one day we had already used up almost half the matching grant. Subsequent donations soon matched the rest of it, and we had well over $100,000 after just a couple months.

As you read earlier, that's when things got really hard. But it doesn't take away from the successful launch this event provided us.

And remember, this is for what is basically a non-existent organization. We did get 501(3) status, and we had a connection to the WPC Nepal program, but Hetauda House as an organization didn't exist before this event, and doesn't exist today. It has no history, no legacy of past supporters, no connections to any businesses or people in the community. Considering that as well as our limited resources, we were quite happy with these results.

Event Lessons Learned – How Much More Could We Have Raised?

An important principle in marketing is to reflect on how things can be done better. And though this event felt like a success, and it was, upon reflection we realized how much better it could have gone. We could have matched the entire grant that night had we made some better choices before the night of the event.

So if you want to do events that are worth all the time and cost they take to produce, pay attention to what you're about to read. This is your Expanded Auction Fundraising Guide with 10 whole lessons just about events.

Event Lesson 1: Debrief your event afterward

We did this, and it's one reason I added this chapter. Especially if you plan to do any events in the future, you need to take time, as a staff, to reflect on what went well and what could have gone better in the one you just did.

In our case, we got feedback saying people felt welcomed. That was good. The dance performance was superb, the silent auction went pretty well, and people gave freely and with joy. But we also quickly realized a number of ways we fell short. Some of the lessons you'll see next came to light in our debrief.

Event Lesson 2: Triple all your time estimates

If you think you can plan your event in one month, give yourself three. If you think it will take three months, give yourself nine. This might be the biggest lesson of them all. The larger the event, the more time it will take to plan, because there are so many details to work out.

And don't trick yourself by thinking that if you just get more volunteers you can cut the time down. No, with more volunteers comes even more work. I once volunteered at a huge event for the Union Gospel Mission. They had probably over 1000 attendees (maybe 2000). They raised over $1 million in one night.

But as a volunteer, when I showed up to learn what I had to do, I was also given a free dinner (not the nicer one the guests received) and lots of snacks I could come back and munch on throughout the evening. Someone had to plan and implement that.

That's a detail, just one of many, that you have to think about with your volunteers. The more on-site volunteers you have, the more work it will be to take care of them. You have to make it clear what they have to do, show them where things are, who's in charge, and all the rest. Helping your volunteers succeed is a big job. And it's just one job of many you have to take care of leading up to the event, and the day of.

You also need table decorations, food and a way to deliver it, a system for collecting people's information, donations, payments for the event tickets, and newsletter signups, a system for running your auctions (silent and live) and other games and raffles, the technology to play music, video, photos and slides, a layout plan for the room, handouts for guests… shall we go on?

Even for a small event of less than 100 people, you will have to deal with most if not all of these details.

I'll say it again – take your number of months for how long you think it will take to plan your event, and <u>triple it</u>.

Ignore this advice at your own peril.

Our event planning failed in this area. And to be fair, we had unique challenges because this was a one-time campaign and a "launch event." We hadn't finalized some of the messaging and other details until within a couple months of the date. We had already delayed our launch date three times because we weren't ready.

Nevertheless, lots of details got pushed back, delayed, or neglected, and these led to lost opportunities. For example:

Event Lesson 3: Have a volunteer meeting – at least 1 hour before the event

This was a big miss. Our on-site volunteers were not unified. They didn't have a clear sense of who was doing what. For example, guests were allowed to serve themselves from an appetizer table. But what happens when a tray runs out? Who's getting the refills? And are we also going to walk around with plates of appetizers to people browsing the silent auction and sitting at the tables?

Then there was a spill near one table, and a mess growing near the drinks. Whose job is it to clean that up?

Your volunteers want to know where things are, who's in charge, and what is expected of them. They need to know how to carry out their tasks, and feel confident they can do so. They need a communication system to handle the unexpected. We could have done a lot better at this. Having a meeting well before the event would have caught some of these flaws.

I'm sure big events probably have this all systematized. But I've seen many mid-size and smaller ones that do not. You've got to plan this well in advance. And whoever is leading that volunteer meeting needs to have all the details worked out well before that, so she can clearly and confidently lead all the volunteers.

As a volunteer myself at multiple events, I can say this: We show up pretty clueless. It's your job to give us a clue. Otherwise we'll be fumbling around feeling awkward all night with no purpose feeling guilty about eating all the food. And, your attendees will feel it, because the event will seem disorganized, chaotic, and poorly planned.

I once attended an event that put 10 people at each table, and they brought out trays of food for the whole table. The trays had 8 pieces of chicken on them. Oops.

Who gets to be the vegetarian for the day? Not I, said the fundraising expert.

Here's the main point: Bad logistics takes your guests' minds off where you want them to be – on your story, and wanting to give.

Event Lesson 4: Put room in your schedule for emotional impact
The worst thing you can do is give a speech that sounds like a high school graduation. Nothing can beat an event speaker who has "been there," wherever "there" is in your organization. Someone who can speak from the heart. Who can connect to the audience.

The problem is, people like this often don't stick to the plan. They may diverge from their notes, or take longer than expected. The emcee might feel like asking a follow-up question.

All this needs to be okay, because emotion is what moves an audience. Not schedules. You need to allow time for this to happen. Time for people to just experience the feelings, to start to empathize. Time to reflect. Time to get to the details.

We did very well at this. One reason I gave the schedule earlier was so you could see our plan and the flow of the event, as well as the rationale behind it.

But notice the times. The documentary, for instance, is 20 minutes long. But we allotted 30 minutes for this. Why? Because the maker of the documentary was going to get up and talk about his experience. He's not a public speaker or a professional fundraiser, and that's a good thing because what he said was from the heart, totally genuine. So we gave him 10 full minutes, and he could have gone longer if he wanted to.

This is about fundraising. We're trying to build a safe home in Nepal, and we need hundreds of thousands of dollars to do it. We need emotion! And it's hard to arouse much emotion in a 2-minute speech.

When you have a speaker like this, the audience will get a lot more out of his talk than anything the emcee or the board president says, because to them, he's "real." We all know the emcee is going to ask for money. That's part of his job. But this guy is just a guy who actually went to Nepal and in the process of filming this, had his own perspectives challenged and transformed.

Give him time, and then give him some more in case he goes over. You don't want him to go on for 30 minutes. But you don't want him to squelch himself because he's worried about going over his piddly little two minutes.

An event that is too scripted for time feels bureaucratic. You want your speakers to be able to get up and be themselves, show their personalities, and connect with the audience.

The raffle-drawing – same thing. You can't just get up and say, "Okay, now we're going to draw the next winner. Give me the dish." You've got to transition. It's a new person on stage. The audience needs time to shift to the new context. Otherwise, they will miss important details you spent months planning, but that get delivered so hastily and in such a scripted way that it feels like a board meeting, which to most people is a "bored" meeting.

A boring event is the surest way to lost donations. Not the only way, but the surest one.

Event Lesson 5: Get a fundraising expert to assess your event plan

We touched on the value of expertise in the last chapter. Here's where it can mean a difference in tens of thousands of dollars.

I attended an event in 2016 that was much bigger than ours. It raised several hundred thousand dollars. But they could have raised so much more had they hired an event-fundraising expert to evaluate their plans.

They were doing a 'raise the paddle' style of auction. This is where you give a number, say $10,000, and ask for anyone willing to give that amount. Everyone who wants to give puts up their auction number. Then, you lower the amount, and ask again. You keep doing this until you get down something like $50.

It's a way to raise a lot of money fast, without needing an actual item to auction off.

But here's the rub. Have you ever heard of 'raise the paddle' before I just explained it to you? Not everyone has. Imagine this is the first ever event you've attended, and the speaker gets up and says, "Who wants to give $10,000? Anyone?"

He gives no explanation. Just asks for this seemingly random amount. Doesn't tell you the process. And then ten seconds later, he cuts the amount down to $5000, again with no explanation.

As a first-timer, you're just sitting there wondering, "What is going on here?" This is what happened at the event I was attending. The auctioneer gave no explanation for the process of how 'raise the paddle' worked, and he moved on to smaller amounts with almost no time to think about it.

For amounts that big, people need some time. Time to consider. Time to ask their spouse who might be sitting there (or might be at home or at work). You can use that time with banter to lighten the mood, maybe give some examples of what $10,000 will buy. A professional auctioneer should know this, and know how to do it well.

But they kept going, way too fast. This was their primary fundraising action for the night. And, this was a wealthy audience, lots of engineers and tech people. They could have raised at least $100,000 more had they conducted this better.

A fundraising expert would have caught this in the plan before the day of the event, and corrected it (or got a better auctioneer).

Here's another area where expertise helps: Table decorations.

Your table decorations aren't there just to look pretty. They're part of your marketing. Figure out a way to engage people and even ask them to give, with your decorations. We didn't just have flowers sitting there. We had cards with stories and photos of kids from the WPC Nepal safe home, and envelopes they could use to give.

Plus, empty tables are boring. Remember what I said about boring events?

If you leave these kinds of details to event planners who aren't directly involved with your organization, they might not think of things like this. You need someone to look at every aspect of your event, and look for ways to inject fundraising and marketing into it. Again – this takes time.

This means your plan and all the details need to be set well enough in advance that someone else can come in and see what's missing – and you'll still have time to correct it.

Get an expert who can find ways to maximize the value of every aspect of your live event. This can mean a difference in tens or even hundreds of thousands of dollars.

Event Lesson 6: Get the most out of your silent auction

Silent auctions are never expected to raise what you'll get in live auctions. But they're easier for people to engage with. They appeal to people who don't like to give in front of large crowds. And they work great for smaller items that fit more people's budgets.

In short – if you don't do a silent auction, you're missing a great way to make your event more fun and engaging for all the participants, not to mention more profitable. Some people never give at live auctions, but they might buy four or five items from the silent one (and the games like raffles).

Our silent auction raised about $1300. Nothing amazing there. But it's $1300 we wouldn't have made if we didn't do it! However, we could have made much more.

Here are seven silent auction strategies you can use to double your profits – with the exact same set of items for auction:

1) Don't set your minimum bids too low

2) Don't set your maximum "buy it now" bids too low – make them at least 2 times the value of the item

3) Pre-set the amounts people have to give at each new bid so they can't raise it by $1 at a time

4) Give enough time for bidding wars to happen – don't start your event too late. You want at least an hour for your silent auction. At least. We only did 30 minutes.

5) Market this – tell people in advance to come early or miss out, and add something special to make them kick themselves if they miss it. Like a silent-auction early raffle, or a free drawing.

6) Have sections of the auction close at different times to build urgency

7) Have people walking around to "talk up" the items that people linger at

That last one is a terrific idea I got from professional auctioneer Laura Michalek (you can reach her at www.lauramichalek.com). I was in a planning meeting with her for a different event, and she hit us with this zinger when talking to us about how supporters can be more effective at getting their friends to give at events.

I tried out her idea.

I had helped acquire one silent auction donation for the event we were planning (not the Hetauda event). The donated item was a one-time fireplace cleaning from a local business I've done some copywriting for. During the silent auction, I noticed an attendee browsing it. A few bids had already been made.

I casually walked up to him, a total stranger, and told him how great this service was, and that I personally knew the business owners. Moments later, he put down a new bid.

Simple, relational, non-pushy. <u>Very effective</u>. Get your volunteers going with this strategy, and your silent auction will explode.

Now, if you've never run a silent auction, you might be sitting there scratching your head. Here's a quick explanation of how it works. If you've done silent auctions before, feel free to skip to lesson #7.

How Silent Auctions Work

A silent auction is like browsing items in a mall. You walk by table after table of items, and you can "buy" any of them. Typically, all the items are donated, either by supporters and individuals, or by businesses who care about this cause or are using the event as a marketing opportunity (or both).

Each item has a value assigned to it. This is the "market value," you might say. For example, one popular silent auction item is an hour in a spa. Suppose a local spa has donated an hour-long session to your auction. They don't get any money for it from your auction. But that hour is still worth what they say it is (note: this also has tax implications for you).

So you, as the event fundraising expert, need to find this out. Let's say they tell you it's worth $100. That means anyone going to that spa for an hour would normally pay $100.

For your auction, each item will have a sheet of paper next to it, and the market value will be on that sheet so people know what it's worth – what they would pay if they went to buy it directly.

Then, you create a chart, and you have a starting bid price. This bid price must be below the market value. A good starting price for this spa might be $30. Maybe $40. You put a box next to that price in the chart, and attendees put their bidder number in that box if they want the spa.

Then, the next row in the chart has another amount. Let's say it's $57. After that comes $73. Then $97. Or something. You have to decide all this. This is what I meant in #3 in the list above about "pre-setting" bid amounts. If someone bids for $40, but someone else wants the item, they have to bid at least $57. If they really want it, they can choose a higher amount, which means anyone else who wants that item will have to bid above them. Make sense?

Some people will want the item no matter what, and will pay almost anything because they also want to support your cause. That's why you also have a "maximum" bid amount, also known as a "buy it now" amount. If a bidder puts their number next to that amount, that item is now off the table and can't be bid on by anyone else.

For this spa, that maximum bid should be at least $300. Why? Because anyone willing to give to your cause who really really wants that spa will pay that much for it. This was #2 in the list above. It's not about the fact they could go to the actual spa and pay only $100. They're doing this to support your cause. That's why they came to your event!

They *also* want the spa, but that's not the main reason they're buying it. You must remember that. At a silent auction, **you have succeeded if all or almost all your items sell for more than the value of the item**. That's a good metric to use. Add up the market values of all the items, and see if the amount you raised is more than that total.

Finally, often a silent auction will have two or three sections, which should be clearly labeled. And it's good to have each section "close" at different times. So, one section might close at 7pm, and the next one at 7:15. Why do this?

Because it builds urgency. When people really want an item, they will keep hovering around that item to see if anyone outbids them. With these deadlines, they know when they've "won" it. And if someone outbids them before the deadline, they'll swoop in and outbid that person before the clock runs out. Using time limits accelerates this behavior, assuming the items are desirable, and increases the chances of silent bidding wars between attendees.

And you want to stagger the closing times of each section because if one section closes, guests know they can still get other items at the other section. You can have bidding wars in multiple sections, all including the same people.

So that's a quick tutorial on how to run a silent auction. If you've never done one before and you're part of a charity that wants to do events, then you just learned something worth way, way more than the price of this book.

Event Lesson 7: Have a floor plan that encourages participation
If your event planner doesn't think like a fundraiser, she might cost you a whole lot more than her fee.

Event planning is a job that requires a particular set of skills. It's a balance of logistics and vision. But *fundraising* event planning piles another layer on top of the normal checklist. It's now not just about the lights, the food, the tech, and all the rest. It's also about how the layout of the venue facilitates or hinders participation, connection, and ultimately donations.

The floor plan is a huge part of this. And here, we lost out.

In our plan, after registering at the welcome desk, guests entered a large room from the right corner. As they entered, they saw a row of appetizers and drinks along the same wall as where they entered.

To their left were two rows of tables for the silent auction items. Beyond those were tables where everyone would sit during the main presentation, with the stage on the far end of the room.

Here's where it went wrong:

With the food basically the first thing you see, the line began to form almost right at the entrance. As more people arrived, the line backed up into the welcome area. This means that people stood in line not knowing what they were waiting for, unable to see anything but a curtain, and the silent auction sat there out of sight, un-perused.

We probably lost an average of 20 minutes per person in terms of the time they could have spent looking over the items in the silent auction. How much money did that cost us?

The more profitable way to do it would have been to make the silent auction tables – with volunteers to answer questions about how it works – be the first thing a guest sees upon entry.

The food should have been placed beyond the auction, so that the only way to get to it is to walk by (or through) the auction items. This is the same reason grocery stores always put the dairy and meat sections in the back. Those are the most commonly purchased items, so they want you to walk through the rest of the store to get to them.

And this way, if a line does form at the food tables, the line will back up *into the silent auction section*.

This is why stores put all the little snacky junk food items and magazines at the checkout stand. You're just standing there, and it's only a buck, so why not buy some Tictacs you had no intention of buying when you came to the store?

It works.

Layout is crucial.

I went to one fundraising event for the Union Gospel Mission that knocked this out of the park. They had a larger venue than we did. But they set it up as a "forced pathway" with everything but one direction shielded with black curtains. This approach allows you to decide what guests see, and in what order. By the time guests even sit down, they are already pre-disposed to give.

First, I encountered a series of displays with huge images and stories – each featuring a person who had been radically helped by this charity. Full color photos, stories to go with them – one after another, four in all.

Before ever sitting down, I had already been moved emotionally in a positive way to see and believe in the life-changing impact of the work they're doing.

Next, I was funneled into the silent auction room, which had rows of tables along the sides of walls. It was huge. And people walked around selling raffle tickets while people shopped.

Only after this did I finally arrive in the main banquet room where the dinner and live auction would take place. Here, I could put down my coat (it was winter), and relax.

See their floor plan strategy? Here it is in three steps:

> 1) Impact you with stories of changed lives. Touch your heart.
>
> 2) Walk you through the silent auction and have friendly people offer food and raffle tickets. Make your night feel fun and exciting.
>
> 3) Send you into the main room to relax after doing a little "shopping." Give you some rest before the main event.

That's a floor plan built to maximize donations.

Event Lesson 8: Set up a system for collecting payments, info, donations – multiple methods

It's all about the information. Remember – marketing an event happens before, during, and after the actual event.

Your system for collecting information and payments must be designed with this in mind (there's that expertise thing again…). Another way to say this is, the goal of registering people isn't just so you can check off your list of who pre-registered and to make it possible for people to purchase auction items.

That's just the basic functionality goal – if you don't have that, your event doesn't work. That's square 1. Any ol' event planner will get that right (hopefully).

The deeper goal is to collect information so you can follow up with additional marketing and fundraising. This is so vital. It's perhaps the most vital part of your event.

Whatever you end up raising that night (in our case, just over $22,000), the amount you can still raise from those people is many times that amount. It's nearly limitless. They might give at future events, or online, or through direct mail. They might become volunteers. They might become peer-to-peer fundraisers for you.

Producing a Successful Event is a Lot Harder than It Looks

Picture this scenario:

A poor college student comes to your event and loves it. But she's a poor college student, so all she does is buy a raffle ticket and one lower-priced item at the silent auction. But her dad happens to know a wealthy business owner.

So she goes home and tells her friends about the event, and then forgets about it a week later. But then, she gets an email thanking her for coming, and how great it was to see her. This email is followed by another a few weeks later, and few more after that. She's not ready to volunteer, and doesn't have any money, but she appreciates hearing about the great work they're doing, and her good memories of that night's event come back in her mind with each email.

Then, months later while at home for the summer, she sees another email, and it reminds her about the event and the organization she learned about. She tells her parents. The email encourages her to tell everyone she knows about their work. She asks if her parents know anyone who might want to support the charity. And then her dad tells her about this newly wealthy business owner who has been looking for a local nonprofit to partner with, but hasn't found one yet.

And <u>that</u> is why you should be doing ongoing email marketing (which you can't do if you don't get the contact information of your event attendees).

Do you see how the chain gets linked together? It's word of mouth. It might take months. It might take years. But you never know who is sitting in your audience, who they know, and who *they* know.

You never know. So if you don't do any follow-up marketing with your event attendees – many of whom are learning about your work for the first time that night because someone else invited them – then you are literally throwing away millions of dollars of potential support.

So here's the same scenario, *without any followup marketing*:

That same poor college student goes back home after the event and tells her friends about it, and then forgets about it week later.

The end.

Which scenario would you rather see happen?

That's why your systems for collecting information exist. That's the real reason. That's why you put response cards with envelopes on every table. Not just so people might throw ten bucks in there. But so they give you a way to connect with them.

That's why you make sure and get everyone to sign in, _with contact information_. Make it part of the process so they have to do it.

Are you worried this might upset people? Don't be. Anyone it upsets wasn't going to stay on your email list anyway, and they can just unsubscribe. You can't worry about offending one person, and lose out on what you can do with ten others. If you're not offending anyone, then you're not marketing right.

Here are some specific elements to include in your registration, signup, and donation process:

1) Multiple ways to register. Online, in person, by check, by credit card, with cash - the more ways to sign up you make possible, the easier it is for more people to get past the main hurdle to come to your event - paying. Once you get them there, then you can impact them. Make it easy to pay and give.

2) Have donation envelopes on all the tables with response cards. Make them part of the event by having the emcee mention them a few times. If you can work out an incentive for people to fill these out, like a post-event drawing, or public recognition, or a free lunch with the founder, then by all means do so.

3) Online registration confirmation at the welcome table. This is just way faster than goofy clipboards. But it's also better because you have it recorded who was there, and you have their emails already - typed, not handwritten. Ever try reading people's handwritten email addresses? Egyptian hieroglyphics are less work, and a lot more fun.

4) Have a separate greeter for people who don't pre-register so they can sign in at the door. Take the time to sign them in electronically and get their emails typed in. Tell them you need their email so you can send their giving receipt for tax purposes. If they don't want to give an email, then ask for their mailing address. Or both – even better.

5) Your CRM system should have an event page signup process. Use it. Salsa Labs made this very easy for us. We set up an event page, with marketing copywriting on it, and then it recorded all the pre-registrants. This is useful for so many reasons I can't list them all. But the main one is, you have a pre-segmented list just handed to you. You can send targeted emails to that list after the event, thanking them for coming, and sending more personalized information.

6) Allow the purchase of multiple tickets at once. Your CRM should make this possible. So instead of buying just one ticket, they might buy three, or six, for family or friends. This is good because people expect it and it's easier for them. But the downside is, now you have only one person's contact information, not six. You need the other five. That's why at the event, you need get the other five signed in as well. How do you justify this? Unless they're all one family, each person needs their own auction number. That's tied to their credit card (or check if they pay by check). Either way, whatever they buy, you need to send them a giving receipt.

7) Have a newsletter signup form – in a different place from the registration table. Why do this? Because some people might slip through your registration system without giving their email. Or they might give a "fake" email - one they never check or that doesn't exist. But it's possible that, as the event goes on, they get so engaged and moved that they decide they really do want to learn more. So, have a table with a clear sign for signing up for the newsletter. You might only get a few names. But just remember the poor college girl. You never know.

The main idea here is twofold.

First, make signing up and checking in easy and fast for attendees, and as flexible as possible. Don't drag out the process. Have enough people checking guests in so the line doesn't go out the door in the cold and the rain (yes, this happened to me once. We were already annoyed before we even got in the room. Not a good giving mindset). Respect your guests well enough to have a fast and easy process.

How many registration volunteers do you need? About 1 for every 50 people is probably a good starting point, but if you can do 1 for every 30, that's a good goal. People don't all show up at once. But remember, this line happens twice. At the end, when guest go to purchase and pick up their auction items, they have to go through the same line again. They didn't all come at once. But they do all leave at once. So have enough people to help.

Second, make the primary goal of every step of this process clear to all your volunteers - to get accurate and complete contact information for follow-up marketing. At the bare minimum, you need to thank everyone for coming and buying auction items. Make sure every volunteer understands this is the most important task they have, and not to let it slide.

How Much Should We Charge For Our Event?

This is a really common question.

This is tricky, because some people get frustrated by having to spend $95 to attend an auction, where they'll be expected to then spend even more. For couples, they've spent almost $200 before even showing up, and then there's the silent and live auction. Before long, only the rich can do this, right?

Well, not so fast. But first, my answer about what to charge is - it depends. That's the answer to almost any hard question, right? In this case, what does your event fee price depend on?

- How many guests you're expecting - size of event
- Cost to put on the event - food, venue, setup, planning, marketing
- Perceived value of your event (often depends on the location, and the history of the organization - but you have some control over *perceived* value)
- How badly you want people to come
- What kind of people you want to come

That last one is a big one. There are political fundraisers, for example, that charge $1000 just to show up. Why do they do that? Because they're going to be asking for far more than that later, and anyone who can't easily pay $1000 isn't going to be able to give at the levels they need so they can plaster us with TV ads and robo-calls for months before November.

You have to think about what kind of giving you need, and how realistic that is based on the people who are in your network.

For example, if you're a medical nonprofit, there's a good bet you'll get a lot of doctors and medical specialists in your auction. Those people have money. So charging them $20 to come to your event actually sends them the wrong message. They expect to pay a decent amount to show up, in part because they'll also expect a higher-quality catered meal and a nice venue.

If you're a fledgling nonprofit with one part-time employee and 35 donors, charging $100 to register might lead to one big empty disappointment.

In the next lesson, you'll read about an event that was free – and almost no one showed up. So yes, you need to charge something. The first goal with this fee is to recover your setup costs so all the money given at the actual event helps you meet your organization's goals (unless you have event sponsorships from businesses).

If you have a low-cost or free venue, you can lower your price. But if you need to charge $50-$75 to recover your costs, and some people complain, just remember – if your goal is to raise $100,000 or more, no one who puckers up at $50 is going to give very much in the auction either. And that's okay. Remember – no one has to give to you. Never forget that. They don't owe you anything. You don't deserve anything, any more than other charities do. They aren't "bad" for not wanting to give more. They might just not be able to afford it.

But this is a <u>fundraiser</u>, not a dinner. You're asking for money. You want people who can give some.

Can we do anything to help people come who can't afford as much?

Yes! If you really want people with lower incomes to be at your event, even though they probably won't buy much at the auction, there are several ways to do this that won't cost you too much:

1) Have an early sign-up discount.

This is such a great and simple idea, I'm shocked whenever I don't see it happening. Even better, have an early price, a regular price, and an extended-deadline price that's even higher. That price will make up for the money you list with the early-bird discount.

And yes, some people will wait until the last minute, no matter how many emails you send them warning about the increasing price. Fine. It's their money.

2) Allow people to purchase groups of tickets or even whole tables

Some people might not be able to afford as much, but their friends or family can. Once they're in the door, most people will end up buying desserts, silent auction items, or live auction items. And certainly raffle tickets. Allow group purchases, and more people can come.

3) Lower your price

Yes, this might be okay, again depending on your circumstances. Just remember that with a lower price, you need lower expenses, the biggest of which are food and venue. You do not want to lose money on your event.

4) Have ticket giveaways.

There are many ways you could do this, and yes, some wealthy person might still win it. But this makes the event seem more fun and desirable, so if you can come up with a good pre-event contest, go for it.

5) Ask them to be a volunteer

Volunteers will still give. And you need volunteers to make your event happen. If someone says they can't afford the fee but really want to come, and you want them to come, ask them to volunteer. You can't have too many of these.

Event Lesson 9: Spend more time marketing the event

If you build it, they still might not come.

One of our heroic Hetauda House volunteers created her own event. One of her strategies was to get a group of local churches to help publicize it to their members. She secured some silent auction items for bidding, planned some food, and arranged with a free venue to show the 20 minute documentary. She did it all. It was meant to be a small event, and she hoped for 50 people or so.

All that work, and not counting the volunteers who were there to help, guess how many people came? Here's a hint: The ____ Amigos.

Needless to say, she was pretty disappointed. Now, the event still raised some money, because the volunteers gave too. But in this case, the churches she relied on for help (and who said they would) gave a pretty uninspiring pitch to their congregations, if at all.

Lesson 9a – if you assume churches will help you because they're churches – they might not. Some churches are already heavily involved in other charitable efforts. But those will usually be honest and tell you that up front. In this case, we got what I like to call a "Northwest commitment." That's because, here in the Pacific Northwest, people are well-known for saying 'yes' to things when they have no intention on following through. But saying 'yes' is easier than making someone feel bad by saying 'no.' So we just lie to them instead, because that certainly won't make anyone feel bad.

Well it does, it's just that you don't have to see the disappointment on their faces, because you've managed to delay it until you're back in the safety of anonymity. Exhibit A: our valiant volunteer who put on this event. (General life advice: Don't lie to people. Have the guts to say 'no' to their face, respectfully.) Moving on….

Why do I tell this story? In part, just to remind you once again that fundraising is hard, and that passion alone doesn't necessarily go very far.

But also because in general, the time you spend marketing directly correlates with the success of the event. This was the one area where our heroic volunteer fell short. And who can blame her? She's working for FREE. But by overly relying on people who turned out not to be reliable, and by not giving enough time to broaden the appeal and interest in the event, the attendance didn't materialize.

You can't ever market your event too much or too early. I say that because **once you pick the date, you should start marketing it.**

People need to be told stuff again and again before they make a decision. Then, they need to be told yet again after they've decided to come, but before the event arrives, because they might forget or cancel. After you've sold someone to register for your event, you need to sell them again to show up.

This is where email marketing comes into play, because it's the easiest way to send reminders, follow-ups, and inspiring messages to build excitement and make your event a true experience, and one to be desired.

And if you have the budget, you should plan for at least one direct mail promotion too – for people who have already signed up for it. Why? Because you really want them to come. Events can raise tens or hundreds of thousands of dollars. Some raise millions. You need "butts in seats," as they say. Don't make the mistake too many make in today's hyper-distracted, commitment-averse culture – <u>do not assume people will show up</u> just because they said they would. Even if they paid a fee.

There are people who buy *Super Bowl tickets* and don't show up. But you think everyone who bought tickets to your fundraiser will be there?

There is much more to marketing an event than we have room for in this book. But the simplest way to sum it up is this: Whatever you've planned to do for marketing, do more of it, and start earlier.

Event Lesson 10: Create a theme

The last lesson on fundraising events is less about practical details, and more about how to sell the event.

Months before you begin any logistical or marketing planning, the first question you need to settle is the most important one of all: What is our event about?

A theme enables you to sell your event as more than just a fundraiser. What sounds more exciting: "Attend our annual children's fundraiser," or "Come to a night of destiny for the next generation." These are made-up of course, so there's no context, but you see the idea. Creating an event theme focuses the attention on something other than the fact you'll be asking people for money.

It connects to your deeper mission and the effect it will have on the world. What are the inner-motivations that move people to take several hours of their time to have auction items pitched at them, as well as all the other activities? You need to tap into those motives, and a theme accomplishes this.

A theme is the hook that tugs on the emotions of their hearts. Emotion gets people moving. Facts don't. Credentials don't. History doesn't.

A theme can appeal to emotion in lots of ways. It can appeal to personal beliefs or values. It can relate to a story. Inspire them with hope. Anger them with tragedy or injustice. Engage them personally. Show them the reality of something that they have the power to change.

There are lots of ways to do this, and at your event, you should use as many tools as you can think of to arouse and engage the emotions of your audience. You do not want them to ask themselves *if* they should give, or *how much* they can afford.

You want them to forget about dollars, and think about impact. It's not money; it's lives changed.

Easier said than done, right? Yes. So put some time into thinking about it. But the first step?

Emotional connection with an event begins with a theme. Your event can be fun, inspiring, transformative, reflective - any number of moods can be created that facilitate giving, participation, and most importantly, fond memories (because they'll be more likely to come back next year and tell their friends).

But a powerful and appropriate theme initiates and sustains all of this. For the Hetauda House event, we called it 'Heirs of Hope.' Besides the huge haul of h's in the phrase 'Hetauda House Heirs of Hope' (alliteration is always a good thing), this theme accomplished a number of goals for us.

First, it points to the people at the center of this - the women and children who will be living in the new safe home once it's built. They are the 'heirs'. The Hetauda House is their inheritance. And by receiving that inheritance and being given the chance not just to live there, but to be educated, counseled, fed, cared and provided for - they also inherit hope. And that hope would be impossible without this new House.

But they also inherit _our_ hope - the hope of the people who give to make this construction project possible. When we give, we hope this house gets built. We hope it saves hundreds of women and kids over the next few decades. We hope it takes people who were abused and destroyed by human slavery, and turns them into victorious conquerors, no longer held down by poverty, illiteracy, exploitation, the caste system, or the other abuses and oppressions they have lived with most of their lives.

Now, don't you feel a little emotion just reading that? Think about it some more, and watch what happens inside you...

When we give, we put a lot of hope into what our gifts will achieve. So the women and kids who live in and get empowered by the Hetauda House inherit our hopes, as well as their own.

All of this and much more gets birthed in the simple phrase "Heirs of Hope." And it's up to the marketers and event planners to capitalize on that theme, and inject it into every aspect of the event they can think of.

Every speaker should talk about it and play off that theme. Graphics and imagery should reflect the ideas within it. With a rich enough theme, even the layout of the event can play into it, and in some cases the very clothing of the participants.

A theme produces the creative spark for all the other elements of your event – including, most importantly, the marketing.

Neglect to come up with a theme (and ideally a new one each year if you do annual events), and you almost guarantee that you'll become stale over time. "Oh, it's that again. Should we go this year, honey?"

That's not the conversation you want supporters to be having. Give your event a new name, with new ideas, and a new vision, <u>every year</u>. Give people a new reason to come.

Does that mean you'll need new logos and graphics? Yes, it does. Do you want to raise $10,000 more than you raised last year? Do you want people to keep coming back, year after year, or slowly drop off and disappear? A theme is that powerful.

A theme initiates emotion. And emotion gets people moving, giving, and promoting your event.

Here are a few things you can do with a theme:

- Layers of meaning. A good theme has an obvious, literal meaning, but it will also have deeper meanings based on which words you emphasize, or imagery it conjures up, or an emotion that can be aroused in more than one way.
- Symbolism. This is one way to bury layers of meaning. Find a theme that expresses an idea through a concrete image that relates somehow to the story you want to tell at your event.
- Pop culture references. Movies, comics, songs, certain celebrities – you can build a whole event around one of these. Just make sure you have permission, if you need it, or find a creative way to tap into the reference without needing permission. "The Force is with us" isn't a copyrighted

phrase, for example. So while you probably can't have the Star Wars logo on your event promotions, you can use phrases like that, and people will still get it.

- Location-based themes. You can build a theme around a famous place, and it doesn't have to be a present-day one. Use history. The key is that it needs to be well-known enough so more than just the two history buffs at your event get the reference.
- Costume or 'dress' themes. Require people to wear certain kinds of attire in keeping with a theme. This can add a layer of fun and exclusivity because it will never happen again.
- Color themes. Sometimes all you need is a color, perhaps one tied to your symbol or layered meanings. Anything that gives your event a visual identity will increase the perceived value.

The theme is where visionary creativity comes in. Whatever you do, you need to find the hook that ties it in to your mission in some way. Then build the rest of the event around it.

Lesson 7 Fundraising Takeaway

Here's a quick review of the 10 Event Lessons for putting on a memorable and profitable fundraising event.

Lesson 1: Debrief your event afterward
Lesson 2: Triple all your time estimates
Lesson 3: Have a volunteer meeting - at least 1 hour before the event
Lesson 4: Put room in your schedule for emotional impact
Lesson 5: Get a fundraising expert to assess your event plan
Lesson 6: Get the most out of your silent auction
Lesson 7: Have a floor plan that encourages participation
Lesson 8: Use a system for collecting payments, info, donations - multiple methods
Lesson 9: Spend more time marketing the event
Lesson 10: Create a theme

Also, send all your attendees a thank you note afterward, either by email or with a mailed note. This is very important, for returning guests and first-timers. Make them feel special and appreciated.

There is no such thing as a simple event. Even a small event with 20-30 people needs all 10 of these items addressed (assuming you have a silent auction, of course) – if you want to raise the most money possible and make your guests happy they came.

If you have a charity that's never done an event, now you have a better idea of what it takes to create a successful one. It's important to have realistic goals, but also not to limit yourself to them.

But it does take a lot of planning. Event Lesson 2 is the most helpful one of all in that regard – triple your time estimates. It will take more time than you think it will. I guarantee it. And though creating a theme was the last lesson, it's the first step. Find a theme, and then build everything else around that.

Lesson 8

Have a Network You Can Tap

THEY SAY, "IT'S ALL IN WHO YOU KNOW." WHEN IT COMES TO FUNDRAISING, that's not entirely true. You need a continuous flow of new supporters, and you're not going to find them all just sitting around the barbecue with your friends.

But if you're setting out to achieve a goal that's far greater than you realistically have any chance of achieving, you will need friends who already trust you and know you. With our little group of semi-paid professionals and volunteers, raising $500,000 in less than a year was, frankly, insane.

But as motivational speaker Warren Greshes puts it (paraphrased), "I hate realistic goals."

Goals are not meant to be too realistic. If they're too easily achievable, then they're not goals. They're just tasks. I don't set a goal to take a shower every day, or brush my teeth. Those are tasks.

For Hetauda House, our initial goal was $250,000, based on the budget estimates we'd been given a couple years before. We thought that was very doable. It was a goal. It would take work. But we were very confident we could achieve it.

A month before we launched our campaign, we learned the budget had doubled because construction costs had gone up overseas. Just like that, our "realistic" goal became $500,000 of trepidation and apprehension. What happens if we only raise $350,000?

But we had come too far to quit. *We had no choice but to succeed.* For our little group, this goal was nearly unfathomable.

We had one thing in our favor, and it was the reason we felt confident about reaching $250,000 (which we reached in just over five months). That point in favor was a healthy network.

We had three branches in our network from which to launch and expand our campaign:

1) Our own church, in which most of the people on our team are members
2) A worldwide group of churches we have relationships with – our project leader especially
3) The WPC Nepal organization, founded by Lila Ghising, which is the program the Hetauda House is built to serve.

Our own church isn't that large. Less than 200 people, many of them poor college students.

But we had high hopes that other churches we're connected with could play a big role in making this happen. If our church can raise $25,000, for example, that's great. If we can get 9 others to do the same, we're at $250,000.

To incentivize this, we created an offer where any person or organization who gives $25,000 will have one of the rooms in the Hetauda House named after them. There are only a handful of rooms in this house, so that's a prestigious opportunity.

Our project leader pitched this to his network in these other churches. And he pitched hard. We also made it as easy for them as possible. We created slides to show their congregations, videos, pictures, and packets with what to say, what to do, and in what order. We gave them a week-by-week plan for how to promote this and motivate their people to give.

All of this took a lot of time for our staff and volunteers.

Lastly, the Friends of WPC Nepal nonprofit gave us their email lists, and we promoted our event and the whole campaign to all of their supporters.

With those three network branches as a foundation, combined with our Ambassador program, we felt that even with the new $500,000 goal, this could still be done.

So how did it turn out? The answer could be considered Lesson 8a.

Lesson 8a: You will be shocked at some of the people who <u>don't</u> give.
Good friends – people we've known for years – did not give to Hetauda House. Some of us got rejected by <u>our own parents</u>. For real.

When you sit down to make a list of people in your life you think you can count on for support, cut it in half, and now you have a reasonable expectation.

It's just like a wedding. When I got married, we were told by all the planners and experts that only about 60% of the people you invite will show up. "Bah!" we figured. "Our friends will come. Most of them live in the same city! What do those planners know? Ours is *different*."

Well guess what happened. About 60% of them came.

And just like Hetauda House, my wife and I were shocked, shocked at some of the people who didn't come to our wedding. We weren't insulted – don't misunderstand – just surprised. The lesson here is simple to grasp yet hard for some people to hear: You just aren't as important to other people as you think you are. (And guess what? They aren't as important to you as they think they are either).

This is a powerful insight, and not just into fundraising, but human nature. We just don't matter as much as we wish we did. I think some celebrities get depressed when they realize this after making millions and achieving a period of fame.

For charities, people have other priorities, concerns, and activities going on. Sometimes, even though they love you, your plans just don't meld with theirs. You have to deal with that.

Our project leader got turned down by some church leaders, people he's known for decades. They turned him down, and didn't raise a dime for Hetauda. He was pretty disappointed by some of these rejections. But that's why I'm putting it in this book. Just like I said at the beginning – *no one* has to give to your cause. No one does. They are not morally, ethically, or even relationally required to give you money.

Anyone who does give is therefore to be thanked and appreciated, repeatedly. Because no one *has* to give. That's why it's called "giving," and not "taxes." The Bible says God loves a "cheerful giver," not ones who give under compulsion. And you as a fundraiser want cheerful givers too, because they're the ones who will happily tell everyone in their lives they support you.

A giver who felt forced to give, or guilt-tripped into giving, isn't going to tell anyone about you. Or if they do, they do so with a sigh of resignation that wouldn't inspire a dog: "Yeah, I gave to them. I just wanted to get them off my back."

So how much did we raise from all these churches?

One church – only one, Grace City in Corvallis, OR – took us up on the $25,000 pledge. Six others raised various amounts less than that. In total, from this branch of our network, we raised nearly $100,000.

That's a great number, and if $250,000 were still the needed amount, that would have gotten us a good chunk of the way. But we needed $500,000.

The flip side of being shocked at who doesn't give, however, is that you'll be equally if not more shocked by who *does* give. Remember those anonymous $50,000 gifts that came in out of nowhere? We were utterly floored by both of them, and both gifts came from people you would never expect.

When you add it all up, you come to a well-known realization that often gets expressed in cliché, but that is nevertheless entirely true: We couldn't have done it without <u>any</u> of them.

Even the kid who put six bucks in our hands at a mostly failed outreach to an arts event – his six dollars helped build this house.

Lesson 8 Fundraising Takeaway

If you're embarking on a big goal, a goal you can't possibly achieve by anything in your own power – you will need a network of people to pursue. And that network will not be enough. But they will give you the confidence to get started. And within that network, or perhaps as a result of someone connected to it, you might just find some additional gems that you couldn't have imagined.

So as you're planning out a campaign, don't feel like you have to start marching in the streets with signs, cold-calling businesses and homeowners, and mailing out anonymous letters to people who've never heard of you. You might end up doing some of those things.

But your plan should most certainly include the people in your network – that means personal, recreational, communal, and even your workplace.

By including them in your plans, you'll have an idea of some of the materials and resources you'll need to create. Because even your friends will need to be given something, shown something, or told to go somewhere to learn more. How will you explain your cause to them? How will you "sell" them?

Once you figure out what to say to people you do know, you'll be in a much stronger position to start talking to people you don't know.

Even though our networks didn't provide as much as we expected, when we branched out in the later months to new territory, we knew our message and had the confidence to pitch it to anyone – including restaurant owners with zero connection to our work and businesses to run.

Lesson 9

Get a Social Media EXPERT

YES, IT'S USUALLY CONSIDERED BAD FORM TO USE ALL CAPS. BUT I HAVE A GOOD reason here. First, the word "expert" has been horribly diluted, with people completing 4-week online programs now declaring themselves experts. You need a true expert. And there are far fewer of those than you think with regard to social media.

I don't care if Facebook has over a billion users. A very tiny percentage of them are true experts at using it to grow a business, or to support a fundraising campaign.

Second, and more importantly in this instance, there's the impression today that everyone is "good" at social media. *Especially* the younger generations. I call this the Great Deception about social media and millennials. I am repeatedly told this every time I protest about technology being too complex and ineffective at living up to its promises. "The kids are all great at it," I'm told.

No they're not.

I was a high school teacher for many years. I saw how "good" kids are at technology when I tried to teach them Excel. Or saw them using a simple word processor or a graphing calculator. They have the same learning curve as the rest of us.

If you want to profit and grow as a result of your social media strategy, you need much more than a college student who knows how to use Facebook and Instagram.

Influence, Not Use

I think the confusion here lies in the difference between knowing how to *use* something verses knowing how to *influence* with the same 'something,' in this case social media.

Here's an outcome every nonprofit wants to see from their social media pages: More people engaging with their pages, and because of that interaction visiting their sites and taking action. But to reach that goal requires far more skill than just knowing how to create pages and post stuff.

Here's another way to think of social media and younger people:

Suppose there's a device that does 50 different things, but 45 of them are very complicated. Most people – almost all of them in fact – are super experts at the 5 simple things, and a portion of them know a few of the 45 more complicated ones.

But hardly anyone is a master of even a majority of those 45 complicated tasks. And the one guy who can do every single one of them becomes an info-marketer and sells his expertise to everyone below him, and becomes a millionaire.

In our society, almost everyone knows the basics of social media. But I have come to know, through repeated frustrating experiences, that *hardly anyone* knows how to utilize the full potential of it. And I include myself in the masses. I hardly ever use social media, and I'm terrible at it.

I've never gotten past the 'iconization' of tech-life where I have to memorize what all these silly little symbols mean, and that there are no directions anywhere, no support, no emails, no phone numbers. Not even a simple diagram or flow-chart that shows me how the various pieces of the system fit together. Not even a welcome or starter kit. Most technology platforms, not just social media, just throw you in the fire and toss a bunch of kindling at you (the kindling being "help pages", poorly searchable forums, and hard-to-read documents with screen caps from older versions that never really answer your real question), and they force you to spend hours flailing around in all that, all by yourself. While your flesh is burning to a crisp.

But that's me.

But unlike me, many people love social media. And yet, they still don't know how to leverage it to do anything useful.

So if you're doing *serious* fundraising and want social media to be a part of it – don't do what almost every nonprofit does:

Do not bring on a college student volunteer to do your social media.

That said, I salute the volunteer college students who took a crack at doing social media for Hetauda House. We had several give it a shot, and they gave great efforts. But take a moment and read between the lines of that statement. This was only a 10-month campaign, and we went through four different social media people in that time.

Why?

Because anyone who gets tasked with *running a social media campaign* – not just randomly posting now and then – quickly realizes this is not an easy task. I'll talk about why in just a bit. But this is probably why our project manager (yes, the paid one) ended up doing the most effective social media marketing we produced.

If you want to use social media to help your fundraising campaign, you will need a marketing plan and at least one person – paid – who is specifically tasked with carrying it out.

For us, we used social media (we stuck to Facebook because of a lack of time and personnel) to achieve several goals:

We marketed our launch event, and sent people to the signup page. We posted blurbs about new blog posts and videos, and sent people to our site to read and watch them. We got a lot of attention, even from Nepal itself. Later, we boosted posts to get more audience, and to inspire more people to give as our campaign neared its goal. We used it to promote the 50k Matching in May campaign.

So we did some good stuff. But we could have done so much more if we had a true expert devoted only to this monumental but so-often under-appreciated task. And that's the most important thing to know about your social media:

If you want it to work, to be a true asset, you need someone who will focus their time exclusively on your social media marketing and management. Not your secretary on her spare time. Not your volunteer coordinator. Not your fundraising director. Not your intern. This is even more true when your traffic starts to increase.

So what can a social media expert do that a typical millennial (or other average user) cannot? What is it that makes this not an easy task?

Here's a quick partial checklist of what you need in a social media expert.

Social Media Expert Qualifications

- √ Able to devote 2 hours per week - bare minimum - with *reliable consistency*, without exception, without having to be reminded
- √ Able to do the work without needing someone else to explain to them the purpose of each post (an expert can recognize the purpose immediately, see the need in advance)
- √ Responds to people's comments appropriately, with a balance of service, fun, and furthering the goals of the organization (this is SO important, especially in fundraising)
- √ Responds to people's comments, period! So many get no response, ever!
- √ Knows how to deliver professional customer service
- √ Knows how to engage people with questions, polls, and quizzes (this requires some tech know-how)
- √ Basic marketing understandings - audience, offer, goal, call to action
- √ Knows which social media platforms are tailored to certain audiences

- ✓ Able to write effective and short copy
- ✓ Understands how headlines, graphics, and calls to action function in the various social media platforms
- ✓ Knows the tools behind each social platform – how that platform best engages its particular audience from an advertising perspective (on Facebook, for example, this means things like "boosting" a post)
- ✓ Understands how social media connects to other marketing channels, both online and off (super important)
- ✓ Knows how to find or create appropriate graphics for each social media platform
- ✓ Can talk about the paid advertising features available in that platform, and ideally knows how to use them already

There's probably a lot more. And notice that some of these items have nothing specifically to do with social media. Yet they are all indispensable if you want this to be an asset rather than an annoyance.

But you're probably wondering something about me – how do I know all these things if I hate social media and hardly ever use it?

The answer to that is why having an expert is so important. I know those things exist, and I understand how they fit into the larger marketing strategy. I don't need to know how to do them in order to know *why* to do them. As the copywriter and strategist, I need someone else who knows how to implement what I know is possible on social media, but that I don't have any interest in learning how to do myself.

I know those needs exist because I have done marketing and fundraising, and social media is almost always the glaring deficit in the plan. Many companies and nonprofits don't have *anyone* doing their social media at all, let alone doing it well.

I've also seen effective social media advertising, service, and maintenance done, so I know what expert work looks like.

Reasons Not to Use College Students, Interns, or Volunteers for Social Media

It's easy to find someone willing to volunteer to do your social media. But the reason they volunteer so quickly is because they have a professional understanding of *almost nothing* on that list you just saw. They know how to use it, but that's all.

Once they realize this is a job and not a pastime, they discover and are quite surprised by how little they know about something they thought they knew everything about. Soon after, they get overwhelmed and suddenly "don't have time," even though they had time when they volunteered and nothing in their life has really changed. Not long after that, you're doing the posts yourself again. Sound familiar?

Social media marketing takes consistent effort and attention. You need someone who goes on your page daily. Daily means every day, and without having to be reminded. They go on and respond to comments and questions. They post. They pose open-ended questions. They inform. They do polls. They find graphics. They bring *value and ideas* to your campaign, rather than waiting around to be told what to do.

You also need someone who responds to your requests daily. If you create a new blog post, or have an infographic you want people to view and share, or launch a new fundraising idea, you need someone who can run with that on social media.

They will need some information from you to do this, like the pages on your site their posts will link to. But they need to be reachable so you can get them to post ads and comments and pictures on a consistent basis.

Social media audiences aren't static. They're constantly moving. Posting once a week, you're likely to hit only a handful of the people following your page.

Your social media expert needs to be keenly aware of your goals, messaging, and strategies. They need to know how their part fits into the overall plan.

Just to be clear: This doesn't have to be a full-time job. But it does have to be a consistent job. Your social media person can't just come in once a week and get all the work done (unless they schedule posts in advance – another example of something they should know is possible and be able to do).

But even doing that, they still need to go on and respond to comments. And not respond the way most people talk on social media:

bad grammer, rong speling. starting sentences with lowercase letters and using no punctuation and using run on sentences and 'textese' "words" like gr8 and lol.

You need a professional. Someone who can WRITE. Someone who self-edits. And perhaps most important of all, someone who understands customer service.

Social Media Is Modern Day Customer Service

People go on to express themselves, comment, and ask questions. It is good service when someone from your organization answers them. When people get served well, how do they respond? They feel good! You want people to feel good about their experiences with you, right?

Suppose someone hears a story that moves them emotionally, so they join your page. They go on and ask a simple question, because they're just learning about you. Four days later, they finally get a response, and it's a one-sentence reply that doesn't really "get" what they're really asking. They may or may not stick around, but you missed your only chance to make a strong first impression.

Have you noticed this about most online communication? People don't talk in an understanding manner. I face this all the time when I need tech support on the various platforms I'm forced to endure.

This is my typical online service experience:

I ask a question. My question, to someone who knows more than me, ought to make them think of not just that answer, but all the other related ideas I might need to consider. And their final answer to me should include all that. "Here's your answer," they might begin, "but if this happens, you might need to do this too. But if this is what you really meant you might need this as well."

That's customer service. Anticipate needs. Empathize. Think about their perspective, and answer in such a way that they will understand and appreciate. This is a skill - and *especially* in today's younger generation that uses too much technology - it is in very short supply. You might be steeped in knowledge about a topic or a particular software, but don't assume the other person is. (Boy, this is good advice for life too…)

What usually ends up happening is that my one question turns into three separate emails, each taking hours to get a response, and a simple problem that could have been *solved in a 5 minute conversation* takes two days. Somehow, I continue to be told technology makes our lives easier and faster. I remain unconvinced.

Customer service might be the single most difficult item to fulfill on your social media expert checklist. But it's so valuable! It's a skill that many businesses find in very short supply. And yes, you can train people, if you have the time to do it or the resources to send them to someone else who does training.

Social Media Fundraising

This lesson is mostly focused on the fundamental need to *have a social media expert*, and less on how that person can support and advance your fundraising goals.

However, since this book is about fundraising, it would be a failure on my part not to talk about this a little. And again, even though I'm not an expert in the use of social media, I know very well what it's capable of doing, and how audiences expect to engage with it.

With that, here are a few tips about social media fundraising:

    1) Directly asking for donations from strangers is a tough sell on social media

This doesn't mean you should never try it. But in general, cold asks of any sort are a tough sell, whether by direct mail, email, social media, or even in person. But for social media in particular, people in general do not go there **intending to spend money**.

This is very important to understand, because this is your audience mindset. Your "buyer persona," as some marketers call it. Whether you're selling something or asking for donations, on social media you are going against the grain of what most people are thinking when they log in.

That said, there's tons of money being spent on social media advertising, and much of it pays off. So what are they advertising if they're not selling stuff or asking for money? Read on.

2) Occupy brains. Get people to engage with your organization

I gave a few examples of this earlier. One thing we did with social media was to remind people to come to the event they had signed up for. This is a big problem. People pay to attend events, but they still don't always show up. Same with paid webinars (and especially with free webinars).

Social media is a terrific way to keep your event on their mind. Email is great for this too. But social media is less intrusive. And this can be done quickly and without upsetting anyone.

Another great use of social media is to draw people to your site. You might want them to read a blog, watch a video, sign up to be a volunteer, take a poll, or many other things. The commonality to all these is, none of it costs the reader anything. So if it piques their interest in the moment, they'll take action.

Why do this? Because it keeps them engaged with you.

The number two job of a fundraising professional (raising money being number one) is to make sure their organization stays on the minds of as many people as possible. The more you stay on their brains, the more likely they are to think of you when they decide to give money or get involved in something.

Use your social media marketing to occupy people's brains.

3) Communicate with people directly

I mentioned this earlier too, but it bears repeating. This is fundraising in its purest form. When someone takes time to comment about something on your page or ask a question, this person is engaging with you. At some level, they care about your work, or were touched by something that was said or done. They might even be upset about something.

The point is, people very often post on social media for emotional reasons. And emotions are what drive participation and giving. So by responding to their comments and questions, you are legitimizing their emotions and making them feel good about expressing themselves. You are validating them.

That's a big deal. That's how you build relationships. And recurring donors – a major goal of almost every organization – happen through relational and emotional connection.

4) Recognize and celebrate people and accomplishments

This is huge too. Social media is terrific for photos and graphics. Celebrate a volunteer's accomplishment. Recognize a peer-to-peer fundraiser who reached her goal. Give a shout-out to the winners of whatever contest you held recently.

Recognition is marketing. Social media is golden for recognition.

5) Educate people in fun ways

Infographics are the most popular way to do this these days, but not the only way. Simple polls and quizzes are fun too.

Finding fun and engaging ways to get people doing stuff accomplishes the all-important goal of staying on their minds, but it also draws them in to your mission and cause. You can make people care if you give them reasons to care. With a direct mail letter, you have to do this all at once. That's why it's so hard for first-time letters to do well. Success usually requires ongoing follow-ups.

With social media, ongoing education is easy. Simple facts and statistics won't move most people to give. But they're really easy to put out there in one sentence posts. Over time, these can "build the case" for your mission. And you can do a lot more in little digestible bites than just give simple facts and statistics.

There are whole books about social media fundraising, so I'll stop here. But notice how much you can do that benefits your mission in the long run, but that doesn't involve asking for money directly. That's the best use of social media for fundraising. It's about connecting with people and building relationships.

That's why most people go on social media. So meet them where they are, and they'll listen to you.

Lesson 9 Fundraising Takeaway

If this lesson felt kind of chaotic, there's a reason for that. Social media marketing, as you have now seen, encompasses all aspects of regular marketing, as well as customer service, and also the ability to use the actual social media platforms. It's technical, it's relational, it's fundraising, and it's marketing. It's complex - and is not a task for greenhorn interns or well-intentioned volunteers.

Here's the most important lesson to take away from all this:

Find your social media expert as early in the process as you can.

This will give you time to train them what they need to know about your organization, who'll they'll be working with, your mission and goals, who you help and serve, and all the rest.

And if you're serious about this, you'll pay them. If you can't afford to pay them, then you need a project manager who understands social media marketing and can delegate to multiple volunteers - not just one. Otherwise, when that one person quits, which they most assuredly will do at some point, you'll have no one except a suddenly overworked project manager to do your social media.

But really, you need to find the budget and pay them. Even if it's just five hours a week. An expert can do a lot with that. A lot more than your project manager.

Use the checklist I gave earlier as a guide to finding a good one. You might be wondering, will we find someone with all those qualifications? If you're banking on volunteers, not a chance. Anyone with all those skills uses them for income (because expertise is in short supply). Your only hope for a free expert is to find a new mom who just had a kid and quit her job as a social media marketer, and is planning to stay home for the duration of your campaign. Yeah…probably not.

But you do have a chance of finding good people with some of those skills. Once you hire them, you can work with them, focus on their strengths, and give them time to build up their knowledge and experience on the other skills they need.

And there are expert freelance social media marketers who don't want to work for big companies. They want a handful of clients who need varying amounts of social media marketing done on a consistent basis. That's your best option. A good one will pay for themselves many times over with increased traffic and donations.

When you hire, the absolute non-negotiable on my job description list is the *daily* commitment. If they can't take 30 minutes a day to go on your social media pages and do basic customer service and simple posting, then they aren't right for the job. Even if they're a volunteer, do not hire them for social media. You're setting yourself up for disappointment. Give them a different task that doesn't require daily attention.

The hard truth is, as I pointed out in Lesson #4 about paid workers, anything that requires ongoing and consistent attention is very hard to any volunteer to succeed in. It's just the way it is. They're volunteers. They have jobs, families, and lives. Volunteerism, in general, isn't compatible with daily commitments.

If you're not willing or able to pay for it, know in advance that you are likely to have weak social media fundraising support. And don't count on it to produce big donations for you. And most definitely, don't expect to have something go "viral."

Lesson 10

Organizational Issues Cannot Be Allowed to Interfere with Fundraising

OH BOY. THIS IS THE ONE THAT CAN GET YOU (AND ME) IN TROUBLE.

First I have to say this: Leadership is hard, in any capacity. Having worked several jobs before finishing college, and in a large public high school for many years after, and for multiple clients in a variety of industries since, I've worked for a lot of people. And unlike some people, I believe in a healthy respect for authority. It's the lack of this that leads to much unnecessary conflict, angst, expense, and wasted time.

However, when it comes to fundraising, there are two categories of people: People who know and do the actual work of fundraising, and everyone else. Some people can be in both categories, depending on how your board and staff are structured. But the people in charge are rarely the people who do fundraising. The best scenario is when both groups know what the other is good at, and empower each other to succeed.

As we learned during the Hetauda House campaign, you cannot ever, ever, ever let organizational challenges get in the way of the most important task - raising the money you need to accomplish your mission.

And boy, did we have some challenges.

Here's a brief rundown of the major ones, followed by a 'bulletproof vest' you can use to protect your fundraising.

Org Issue #1: No Contract

We began our campaign in September of 2015. By March of 2016 - three months before the campaign ended - we still had no construction contract. In fact, we didn't even have a *company* to create a contract with, because two of them had dropped out. When your entire campaign is about constructing a new house...

Having no contract or construction company is a BIG problem!

And this was not for lack of effort. Here's some timeline stuff to give you context:

In 2012, a group of men went to Nepal, filmed the documentary, cleared the land where the Hetauda House now stands, met the children and women in the safe home, and had what are commonly but not incorrectly referred to as life-changing experiences. Their worlds got rocked.

(And they were all men, in case you're wondering, and for a specific reason. These men wanted to do something to combat the abuse that so many women and girls face around the world, and they recognized that it will take *men* to stand up against the crime of human trafficking, if it's ever going to be stopped. This is because men are most often the ones committing and facilitating these crimes. I say this because I agree with it, and because these men are heroes for actually doing something instead of just talking about it).

All that to say, 2012 would be the ideal date to pick if you wanted to mark the true beginning of the Hetauda House.

From that time, the never-ending question of "what next?" drove those men forward. We need a website. We need a logo. We need a plan to raise money. We need a building plan and blueprints. We need a bid.

Between 2012 and 2015, these sorts of questions were being raised and answered.

I say all this because, sometime during these years (I wasn't involved yet), they got some construction estimates, and identified a handful of Nepali companies they could call on for bids at the proper time. These were the bids that got shockingly revised to nearly twice the original amounts right before our campaign, as I have described previously.

We had a preferred construction company we were planning to use because they had also helped with the designs. And even with their higher bid, we still had the green light. All that remained was to finalize the contract.

Sounds easy enough, right?

The first problem was distance. Our fundraising group is in the U.S. The companies are in Nepal. The actual workers in the WPC Nepal safe house were not directly involved with this project. They are busy caring for the women and kids in their existing program. So we had no on-site liaison to help mediate and forge this contract with the construction company. As I'll share in a bit, we later got such a person, and this person eventually got the contract.

But would you believe we actually raised all $475,000 for the Hetauda House construction without a signed construction contract in place? It's true. In fact, they didn't sign the contract until the day before they broke ground.

Do you see why this is an organizational problem?

We're telling people who are giving money, large sums of it in some cases, about this house thing we're going to build in Nepal. And not only do we not have a contract, but until March or so, we don't even have a company to make a contract with!

So how did we handle this? We handled it the only way we could, because we put our fundraising first, and weren't going to let this interfere with it: We kept it to ourselves, for the most part.

Quite frankly, our donors didn't need to know all this. For one, it would be impossible to communicate it in such a way that everyone will understand it and not have any problems, questions, suspicions, or even worse, apprehensions about giving.

And for two, we knew this would eventually get worked out. It was a nightmarish headache for our tiny little team and frazzled project manager, but we knew it would get worked out. It had to. We just didn't know when, how, or what we would do if it all fell through again.

Now to be clear, there was no veil of secrecy. If people asked, we told them what was happening. But we didn't make this a part of our official communications with supporters.

1st Bulletproof Vest for keeping organizational issues from affecting fundraising: **Keep them internal.**

Org Issue #2: Companies Dropping Out

Talk about an emotional roller coaster. Remember earlier when I mentioned how hard things got in Feb – March of 2016. This was one of the main reasons, and our team fell into a deep, dark February funk. It was not good.

The first construction company we had planned to go with dropped out unexpectedly for reasons I'm still not clear on. By this time, we had our liaison in place, and he re-bid the project with other companies, and found a new one. This was great news!

But then, a little while later, that one dropped out too, deciding to pursue another project, and they didn't have enough staff to do both.

By this time, *we had told our donors* that we now had a construction company lined up. Oops.

Nothing dries up donor confidence like hearing that there's no construction company for your construction project. And when our liaison in Nepal heard that we had not only told our donors about an agreement with the second company, but we had *named* them publicly, he was "unhappy," to put it mildly.

So, when he found a third company that said they could handle this project, we didn't want to get too excited about it. Plus, we were so demoralized at that time that it was tough to think positively. But we also had to deal with the fact we had let the cat out of the bag on the second company. Donors were asking questions about progress. We can't lie to them. So whenever someone asked, we'd just tell them that second company had dropped out, and that we were pursuing a third one.

You just reassure them as best you can, be honest, and remind them that you have a strong team on the ground that won't stop until the deal gets done.

Then, you refocus donor attention on the people - the women and kids in our case - who will live in this home as a place of refuge, restoration, and renewal.

Plus, we also knew that with money in the bank, *some* construction company had to emerge from somewhere. This wasn't an idea in our heads. We are ready to build, and we've got the dough.

Nevertheless, though we were at a low point, we did not let our challenges invade or interfere with the story we continued to tell our supporters. They need to know what is going to happen, not about the complications that are in our way.

2nd Bulletproof Vest for keeping organizational issues from affecting fundraising:
Focus on the end goal, not the present

Org Issue #3: No Construction Budget

Are you starting to see why this was so hard? All these things are happening simultaneously, and they're all related. With no contract, and no company, we also therefore had no finalized budget.

But in fundraising, one of the most basic strategies for a singular project is to set a goal, promote it, and then celebrate when you reach it.

It's kind of hard to set a goal when you have no official costs.

Initially, we thought the costs would be $250,000. Then, they got revised up to $500,000 based on the current construction costs in September of 2015. But that was still a projection, and it was from a company that dropped out of the bidding a few months later.

As the months went on, we heard wildly fluctuating numbers coming from Nepal. It's $470,000! No, it's down to $413,000! No wait, now it's like $450,000! Okay no... now we think it's $475,000! Actually, it might be *over* $500,000! What? Are you serious?

It was like the stock market during a political campaign.

You might think I'm joking. And you would be wrong, sadly... The numbers kept changing because we wanted numbers, so our Nepal liaison kept sending them to us. But his numbers took so long to finalize because of all kinds of technical stuff that no one ever thinks about unless they're in the construction business.

Soil core samples. Concrete testing. Company negotiations. Combing through the plans to find cost savings. Combing through the plans to increase the earthquake resistant features. Combing through the plans just because. Getting a new comb. Materials. Staffing. Timing. Weather. Contingencies. Arrghh!

Paraphrasing Dorothy from *The Wizard of Oz*, "Core samples and cost savings and contingencies oh my!"

All silliness aside (and at some point, you do have to just laugh during times like this), this was *incredibly* frustrating for everyone. You feel totally powerless. It's all happening way over in Nepal. There's literally nothing we can do to make it go any faster or get any clearer.

And bringing it back to donors – what in the world do we tell them about the costs?

Organizational Issues Cannot Be Allowed to Interfere with Fundraising

What happens if it ends up being more than $500,000? What if we raise that much, but then it ends up being a lot less, like the $413,000 we heard at one point? That was an easier question, because the building also needed interior furnishings, computers, and other items donors would easily rally behind and be thrilled to have provided.

Nevertheless, it's very hard to focus donors on the end goal when you don't actually have….a goal.

So what did we do?

We tried, as best we could, to not broadcast all these chaotic budget vicissitudes, or the reasons for them. Again, this is internal stuff. The number will settle at some point. And for the great majority of the campaign, we were nowhere near $500,000, so we weren't too worried about having too much money.

But here's what you need to get out of this: Donors don't care about core samples or contingencies. They don't want to hear about complications and frustrations – however real they might be. You must keep your work separate from *their perception* of your work. You must, especially when you interact with anyone who doesn't already know about all these organizational frustrations, try to speak favorably about the work you're doing. Cast it in a positive light. Find the sunny side.

I don't mean be fake. I just mean, the people you talk with will talk to other people. You don't want to sow an undercurrent of presumption that your entire campaign is about to implode. That's not good. You don't want to give the impression of internal chaos, or that no one knows what they're doing. This takes the focus off your impact, which is what donors care about. And you will sow these negative beliefs if you're constantly venting or fuming or unloading all your stress on anyone who asks.

How do you keep a healthy balance for yourself without blabbing about how it's all a big mess?

3rd Bulletproof Vest for keeping organizational issues from affecting fundraising:
Confide in a few trusted friends, or within your team, to process frustrations

Addendum to 3rd strategy – <u>Never</u> vent about your organizational issues on social media. Ever.

Org Issue #4: Cross-Continental Communications

As I mentioned earlier, we teamed up with Construction for Change (CFC), a non-profit that specializes in construction projects in developing nations, to help us facilitate the actual project in Nepal.

The liaison I keep mentioning is from CFC, and he did a tremendous job. Part of CFC's unique approach is to send project managers with experienced construction backgrounds, and they actually live on site while their project gets done.

Our CFC representative, Marcus, moved to Nepal in April of 2016, and lived there for over a year. They also sent other people over at various times to appraise the project, work the ever-evolving bidding and budget process, and other tasks.

But Marcus saw the project through from start to finish. He succeeded in securing the final bid, negotiating the contract and the finalized plans, and overseeing the actual construction. He also took photos throughout the process and sent them back so we could keep donors updated and excited.

While he was in Nepal getting himself established and getting started, we quickly realized the many challenges we would face in communicating with him.

For one, it's the simple time zone issue. He's halfway around the world. When he's asleep, we're awake. So just basic communication takes longer than you'd like.

He's also dealing with cross cultural issues on his end. On our end, we've got multiple people talking to him all wanting various kinds of information. Plus we had to negotiate his housing (which was much harder than we initially had expected) and other personal arrangements.

The biggest challenge, though, came from the fact that he was so busy working to get this project going, that sometimes it would be weeks without a word. It's just not easy to work through situations like this. I wasn't directly involved with this part, but I did hear a lot about it from the project manager.

I think everyone was doing the best they could, and in the end it worked out. But we had some interpersonal challenges, miscommunication, poor assumptions, and other frustrations that occasionally raised a few hairs, probably on both sides of the ocean.

But what did we tell donors?

We told them how much easier this project was going to be because of our alliance with Construction for Change, because they'd make sure this project gets done the best it can possibly be done, at the lowest costs possible. And that was completely, 100% true.

In other words, CFC was an asset, a bonus, a plus, a blessing, and a big win for Hetauda House. Donors were thrilled when they learned about CFC joining our project, and they stayed thrilled about it throughout. We never told them about these internal challenges. Why not? Because this isn't reality TV, and we don't need to air our junk.

And neither do you.

4th Bulletproof Vest for keeping organizational issues from affecting fundraising: **Do not speak ill of anyone who's on your side when in the donor's earshot.**

(And yes, that again means social media – especially!)

We had many other organization-level challenges come our way that I won't go into here, including one that caused more problems than all four of these combined. But the most common problems are simple disagreements within staff, which will happen everywhere at some point.

The four Bulletproof Vests I've given so far should protect your donors from being damaged from any internal challenges that come up. Here they are once again:

1) Keep them internal
2) Focus on the end goal, not the present
3) Confide in a few trusted friends, or within your team, to process frustrations

4) Do not speak ill of anyone who's on your side when in the donor's earshot

In addition, here are six more Bulletproof Vests to help you prevent non-fundraising challenges from impairing or torpedoing your mission:

5) Know your mission

To stay focused on your mission, everyone on your team needs to know what that is. Our mission was to fund and build the Hetauda House. That was always the goal, and we never wavered. No matter what strong winds came against us or from which direction they came, our team kept working toward the goal.

6) Have a committed staff who understand the priorities

Your staff needs to be clear on priorities. Number one is never to work through the details of a contract or to resolve communication challenges. Those are important, but they are never the top priority. Help your team keep challenges in perspective.

7) If you have to put something off, put off the organizational stuff

This relates to #2, but it bears elaboration. Sometimes you just don't have enough time. If you need to finalize a presentation for a group of potential donors tomorrow, and then someone calls about a volunteer conflict that just erupted, what do you do, if you don't have time to address both challenges?

You finish planning the presentation. Donors are your lifeblood. You can sort out the other issues later. Yes, this goes against our 'instant-everything' culture, and is massively offensive to most millennials (yes, I've seen it in person), but just about everything that's interpersonal can, in fact, wait.

8) If you have to prioritize time or expense or people, prioritize for fundraising

It's hard to make this particular generalization because I'm sure there are exceptions (and these are all generalizations, by the way – human wisdom should always be applied in any situation, which is why good leadership matters so much). But here's what I mean:

What should you spend money on if you have to choose? Next month's email campaign, or a new computer for your secretary? I know it's a context-less scenario, but unless the computer is expelling noxious fumes and there's no temporary replacement even if it's a face-whitening two years old, you spend first on the email campaign.

What does it mean to 'prioritize for people'? Again, dreaming up hypotheticals isn't very fun, and there are millions of possibilities. But a staff member's complaints are less important than a donor's questions. Thanking a donor is more important than thanking your team (I'm not saying don't thank your team!!).

Is this making sense? As scenarios arise, keep fundraising at the forefront as you work through internal challenges. At the same time, a healthy staff will produce better fundraising. Good relations with the board will produce better fundraising, because it will mean less turnover.

Internal stuff matters - a lot - so please don't misinterpret what I'm saying. But donors - real people - are literally handing you their hard-earned money, and asking nothing in return.

That selfless act, and the tasks you need to be doing that relate to it, come before all else in your mission.

9) Do not let "time-suckers" steal your mojo

I had to say it. Some people just love to "process." At some point, it's time to act. Don't debate your mission statement for the 20th time this year. Quit word-parsing every sentence of an obscure page on your website that two people are going to read (i.e. trust your copywriter!).

Some of this goes back to the expertise lesson. I could summarize it this way: Don't let non-experts slow down the execution of important tasks. You only have so much time, and it's never enough. If someone is sucking away all your time, figure out a way to 'muzzle' them nicely, because you just don't have time for it.

10) Demand non-fundraisers do their jobs - what they promised to deliver

You can't make people give you money. But you can, and you should, make people do what they promised.

In our case, Construction for Change made certain promises to us, and we even worked out a detailed contract that took many hours to negotiate. Partnering on a construction project is not a small task. But once that contract is in place, both sides can now use it to keep the project moving.

But this also applies to people helping out with events, vendors who promise to deliver something by a certain date and with certain details correct, volunteers who commit to showing up or doing something that you're depending on them to do, and many more situations.

Your staff will probably always be overworked and underpaid. That's the nature of the business. But they do it because they're committed to your mission (#5 and #6).

What they don't need is other people failing to follow through on things they have agreed to do. Obviously you can't force someone to do anything. But in that event, you just make a decision not to do business with that person or company again, and politely end the relationship – no matter how long they've been working with you.

Your fundraising and mission are at stake if you don't.

I once worked on a project with a paid web developer. And the developer would take weeks sometimes to respond to questions or revision requests. Weeks! And they were paid (that means, supposedly, an expert). What should have taken a week or two ended up taking months, and in my opinion, still didn't get done right. Were I running that organization, I would never do business with that developer again.

Lesson 10 Fundraising Takeaway

Hopefully you have gleaned the common theme behind all ten of these Bulletproof Vests – *only tell donors and supporters what they need to hear to stay positive and motivated about the work you're doing.*

Organizational Issues Cannot Be Allowed to Interfere with Fundraising

Whatever organizational challenges you might face, you should work through them with that as your guiding principle.

I said at the beginning that this is the lesson that can get you in trouble. And while none of my examples really related to leadership, because by and large our leaders were solid all the way through, organizational issues very often arise as a result of leadership issues. And sometimes, you'll have to fight hard to keep the message positive and donors at the center of your priorities.

Disagreements can come from all sorts of places, from tactics, to priorities, to personality, to who does what, to compensation, to all sorts of other things you know well already.

And this book isn't about how to work through staff challenges. But the core lesson remains, no matter how bad things look from the inside:

Donors and supporters do not need to see your dirty laundry.

Lesson 11

No Substitute for Thorough, Clearly Presented Information

IF A HOMELESS PERSON ASKS FOR A DOLLAR, HE HAS A REASONABLE CHANCE OF success. If a nonprofit asks for ten dollars, it has a reasonable chance of success too, even if it gives very minimal information (though, even $10 can be a lot harder than you think!).

But when trying to raise $500,000 in ten months to build a 5-story facility on the other side of the world, it's going to take more than a "please give" sign and a ringing bell. Not that there's anything wrong with that.

As fundraisers, we can never forget the people at the center of all our plans – the donors. These are our audience. In marketing terms, a potential donor is a lead. And leads don't buy without an emotional impulse and a reason to back it up. Marketers say it this way: People buy because of emotion, and they justify it with logic.

That's a profound truth that applies to almost everything you buy, from organic food (no, it really isn't "better," but people have justified their emotional desire for

No Substitute for Thorough, Clearly Presented Information

it by coming up with some logical reasons that work for them) to cars, to technology, to clothes, to just about anything.

Donors fit this model perfectly. No one gives for rational reasons only. They give because something about your cause twitches their emotions in such a way that they decide to help. They care. And that's a good thing.

But caring isn't enough. Because given enough time and media, anyone can find a dozen different things to care about, and all of them need donations. And this where the 'logic' piece comes in. You have to make them care enough to give. That's your first task. But then you have to help them justify their decision with clear information - the logic that backs them up.

I always liked this analogy: If one spouse buys something (or donates), what will they say to help their spouse be okay with it? The person buying buys for an emotional reason. But their spouse may not share that emotion. The spouse needs logical reasons before they will go along with it. So the 'logic' isn't just for the buyer (or donor). It's for the other people in their lives who might need some convincing too.

When you provide good information, *you're giving your donor the selling points* to use with their spouse or significant other to justify their decision to give to your cause.

Make sense? This is why clear information that your donor - and their skeptical spouse - wants to know is so important. It's why when we design a website and a campaign, we must do it from the donor's perspective, not just our own. Almost every nonprofit website falls short in this area.

Poor clarity is especially common in smaller nonprofit sites. They have one page, lots of pictures, hardly any text, and they want me to give to something I barely understand. Only people who already know about the issue will give to that. The rest of us will look it over, give it 30 seconds or so, and move on.

If you want to cultivate real donors - real supporters who will get passionate about your cause - you need clarity. You need a functioning giving process. You need information that answers questions, addresses doubts, assures legitimacy, and ignites passion.

What Do We Have?

I love the scene in *Austin Powers* where Dr. Evil finds out his underlings weren't able to procure the sharks with laser beams attached to their heads, because they got caught up in red tape and animal abuse allegations. After he goes off on a tirade about this, he asks a simple question: "What do we have?" The answer? Ill-tempered sea-bass. Right.

When I came on board the Hetauda House team in December 2014, that was my first question: What do we have? It became evident almost immediately that we had already committed a grave mistake – we were doing this in the wrong order. Here's what we had:

We had a very rough plan to pursue a peer-to-peer fundraising strategy, but no way to implement it. We had Lila's founding story written out, but it was very hard to read because the site design was so dark. We had a good tagline – Building Hope for Nepal. And we had the 20 minute documentary and some trailers for it, on which the success of the entire campaign depended, a mistake we explored back in Lesson #2.

There was almost no other information available on the website or elsewhere. No way to get questions answered other than filling out a form and hoping an anonymous volunteer or drastically underpaid worker will write back. All the site had was the documentary, a request to give, and some generic information about human trafficking.

In spite of that, this website cost *several thousand dollars* to build. Important micro-lesson: While you need to invest in expertise, it's also possible to waste your money. That's why you need someone who understands campaign fundraising and all its components to help with planning your strategy *before* you go out and spend thousands on specific needs. It has to be done in the right order.

Clear Information Rule #1: Do It in the Right Order
This is the right order:

1) Specify your goal

2) Create strategic plan

3) Develop core messaging and copywriting

4) Design website and materials

5) Initiate campaign

In building a website when we did, we skipped from step 1 to step 4 (an all-too-common mistake I encounter frequently). Thus, we ended up with a website without a plan or a message. And we would not have raised $475,000 had we not re-worked it before launching the campaign.

Using that process, we already had the goal. At the time, we wanted to raise $250,000, but as you've read, this number continued to shift for months, even after launching the campaign. While the exact number was not known, the ultimate goal was clear – build the safe home facility.

Next up, the strategic plan. To create this, you need to answer a number of questions that *donors will ask*. Since at this point in 2014 we were mostly focused on the website, I'll deal with that for now. Here are some questions a good fundraising site needs to answer for potential donors:

1) What is this organization about?

2) Why do they need money?

3) What does my money accomplish?

4) How can I get more information?

5) How well does their stuff work?

6) What do they do?

7) Can I trust them?

We could come up with many more specific ones for individual sites. But in general, on every website, the first thing people ask themselves is, "What is this, and what do I do?"

If you can't answer that quickly, you will lose them. It also matters what they may have already seen or heard before coming to your site, such as an email from a friend, a direct mail letter, a PPC ad, or a table at an event.

A well-written headline and introduction can answer almost all those questions. But online, the key is to make it easy for people to do question 4: How can I get more information? If whatever they've seen on that first page isn't enough to satisfy their need for answers to any of these questions, how do they learn more? Where do they go? Who can they talk to? And is it <u>easy</u> to do all this?

Having information, but making it impossible to find – that's called poor usability.

Having no information – that's called insufficient planning.

Having too little information and no easy way to find what's there amidst all the massive pictures – that's called modern graphic design.

A Graphic Design Commentary – Design is not Information

Why did it cost so much to build this site if it wasn't going to serve our needs? This is an important question, because every website needs design. And good design is harder to come by than you think in our squarespace-wordpress-instapage world. A lot of designers are clueless about marketing.

A GKIC marketing newsletter quoted the Chief Marketing Officer of the Proactiv® acne treatment brand. This is a billion dollar direct response marketing business. They know a few things. Asked what it takes to design a good website, he said, "The three things you need for successful website design are a legal pad, a pencil, and a knowledge of how to sell." I love it. Everything else, including the actual design, is just details. Important details, to be sure. But it's not where you start.

If certain organizations put half the effort (and investment) into real fundraising marketing as they do in their "brand," they'd be rejoicing with all the increased donations.

In our case, we spent a lot of money on the web design and the visual theme, with almost no content strategy or consideration for the needs of donors and visitors. It was designed without a workable plan to raise the amount of money we needed.

When the Salsa advisor I spoke with first saw our website, he was baffled that we expected a single documentary – and a 20-minute one at that – to be enough to raise the money we hoped to raise.

So let's get clear on a couple things about web design. It costs money, as it should. It's a specialized skill; I certainly can't do it. It takes a lot of time to do well. But in general, web designers do best when someone else tells them what's needed in terms of the strategic plan. They can cost you thousands if you give them free reign, and the end result might accomplish almost none of your goals. I've seen it happen many times. And I've had real designers confirm this to me. They aren't strategists. They are *implementers* of strategy. Know the difference.

The way you can tell this is true is because, very often when you first sit down with a designer, their first question will be some variation of this: "So what ideas do you have in mind?"

This is not a dumb question. This is a question asked by someone who wants to be given a place to start. From there, they can do their thing, and the good ones do it very well. But strategy defines design. Your marketing and fundraising strategy dictates graphic design. I cannot stress that enough. Design does not define strategy.

Here's a simple example: If you're setting up a brand new site (like we were), what will you put in the menu navigation? That menu navigation, something every website has in some form, is part of your strategy, and the designer cannot tell you what to put there. Thus, without a marketing strategy, your designer is in the dark even on a detail this routine.

Did you know big companies spend tons of money testing their menu labels, among many other details? They'll change just one word and then test how it affects site engagement. This stuff matters. You can't just vomit up a website and expect people to give.

Look at this list of six major problems on our site, and think about these from the perspective of a donor trying to answer those seven questions I listed earlier.

How Bad Design Affects the Donor

1) Unreadable text

It had white text on a very dark background, and the only other page of content on the site had very large font stretching across the page. You could barely read it. How will a potential donor react to a site they can barely read?

2) Senseless menu navigation bar headings and design

This was a big problem. For one, each menu item just pushed the visitor farther down the main homepage. None of them actually went anywhere. This is a major flaw I've seen on other sites too, and it makes no sense at all.

Navigation bars only have so much space. This method of design uses that space just to take people farther down the same page. What's the reason for this? Why would I want to click on 'Share' if I haven't learned anything about the program yet? Never mind that I have no idea what 'Share' means, or if I want to do it, or where it will take me. But if I do click on it, I will be even more confused, because it will shoot me down the page to a panel that tells me nothing useful, and gives me no reason to want to 'Share' this page with anyone else.

'Share' is one example of a Hetauda House menu bar that was filled with poor and worthless labels, all with vague meanings, such as 'Watch,' 'Dive Deeper,' and 'Join Us.' What does it mean to "join"? What are we joining? Nobody knew (and yes, I asked).

When we re-strategized the site, our new plan included helpful and specific menu labels, such as 'The New House', 'Our Program,' and 'Get Involved.'

In the grand fundraising scheme, this is a small thing. But really, it's not small at all if you're thinking about donors, and not your own cleverness. If a donor wants to learn more about the Hetauda House so she can tell her husband how awesome this new building will be, *can she figure out where to click?*

That's a far, far more important question than what color to make your background.

3) No dropdown menu option – template disallows it

Why designers feel the need to do these sorts of things continues to escape me. Even if you don't want a certain feature right now, who's to say you won't want it later? Sites change all the time. Nevertheless, someone built the template code to make dropdowns impossible to add to the navigation menu. Someone went *out of their way* to disable a feature that is standard (or should be) to website templates.

So we couldn't do dropdowns. Apparently, dropdowns were "out" that year, in spite of never losing a bit of their usefulness for donors. And since the people who designed it created this site three years before, they were unreachable (another common problem with designers – not so different from subcontractors for real construction projects). Only the site's creators had access to certain key php files. In non-tech-speak, this means we couldn't fix stuff like this.

Why are dropdowns nice to have? Well, which is easier: To click on 'Our Program' and see a few categories drop down showing the different parts of the WPC Nepal program, or be forced to click on the only option you see and then hope that page has what I want?

Me? I like the dropdown option. It's easier. I don't have to click as much. Other people like the second option. To each their own. What's the point? We can do BOTH! We don't have to pick only one way. And good usability helps as many people engage with your site <u>in the manner they prefer to do</u>. Too many designers either don't understand that, or just thumb their noses at it and do what they think looks better.

Technology is supposed to make things easier. And we have the technology that can make things like this easier. But so often, we forcefully refuse to use it because of some misguided belief about what "looks good" or what's "trending" in design, as if newer is always better.

In other words, we have the power to design this in a way donors will benefit from, but we choose not to because we think that kind of site is out of style. Is that smart fundraising? Not on my planet.

   4) No buttons allowed – template disallows it

Noticing a pattern here? I could go on for pages about all the things the template disallowed or made very difficult. But no buttons? No buttons??? Seriously? I am not making this up. We could not put a 'Donate' or 'Give' button on the home page of a nonprofit site that wants people to donate and give.

Our tech volunteer, who does this for a living, had to do a crazy workaround to get a button on there. And he could only put it in certain places, not where I really wanted it. He assured me the traditional (meaning – simpler) route to creating buttons couldn't be done without access to files we didn't have access to because the creators had vanished. I was utterly dumbfounded. Why would you make a site in such a way to make buttons *impossible* to add?

Again, this is what can happen when a designer gets to set your website's *strategy*. Does the foreman on a construction team tell the architect how to plan out a new building? The foreman is the implementer of the architect's strategy, just like the web designer implements the copywriter/marketer's strategy. Do it in the right order, or your building will fall down.

   5) General absence of basic home page flexibility

I wanted to add buttons. I wanted to change the color of the 'Give' link on the navigation bar. Or the size. Or both. I wanted options! "Can't do it because of the template" I was told over and over.

I had never seen a site so restrictive to adaptation and adjustment. And again the simple question is, "Why?" How does this help the donor? It doesn't.

   6) Incompatibility with external payment sites

We purchased Salsa Labs, as I mentioned back in Lesson #3. One of their features is branded donation pages – a huge asset over generic ones like Paypal and Network for Good.

Part of the process of enabling Salsa required us to use our website to create templates for the pages we'd be hosting on their site. But when they started taking our code to make their templates, it was a disaster. It took multiple rounds before we finally got it to work, lots of frustration, and a lot of wasted time. The main culprit? You got it. Our inflexible web design created before we had a plan. This template was still causing us headaches even after it didn't exist.

A process that should have taken a few minutes took days of haggling with Salsa's tech support. But it wasn't Salsa's fault. It was bad design.

A Helpful Perspective on Web Design

A great analogy for websites is to think of them like a building. I credit this analogy to renowned copywriter Nick Usborne. Buildings have walls, rooms, floors, pipes, wiring, appliances, windows, and all the other internal and structural elements that make a building function. Without these, it's a condemned and worthless blight. Buildings also have paint.

When you build a house, the paint is the last thing you do. And it's important. No one buys a house without paint. And paint protects the surfaces, as well as beautifies it.

Likewise, without effective web design, people can't engage with your site. Design optimizes usability, which is essential to all your marketing pathways.

Some web designers might object to my strong language in this section. But I've worked with a lot of them (or been forced to labor in the aftermath), and I've met only two who operated from a *marketing* design perspective – Blue Ivory Creative being one of them. And no, I don't get paid for mentioning them. I just like commending quality.

In general, designers are implementers, not marketing strategists. And again, this is not a criticism. It's a clarification of roles. Designers *want* to be given direction. They thrive when given a clear place to start, a goal, and a strategy to get there.

What did we do with our unworkable website?

First, we scrapped all the content and developed a new site strategy (this is step 2 when you do this in the right order). Then, based on that plan, I wrote all the content (step 3). And from there, we then redesigned the site (step 4). Through much duress since we still had the same clunky template, we got it to work.

One problem with all this - with a small campaign like ours, who has the money to spend on all this development? And you have even less time than you do money. What we ended up eventually doing, many months later, was to scrap the entire site - including the template - and start from scratch.

Two volunteer tech guys (again, unemployed at the time) spent many hours and days creating a whole new version. It was brighter. You could read it. Updating with the latest news was easy, as it should be. This is the version we should have had throughout the entire campaign.

In the building analogy, what we had to do was like remodeling. Someone put up the paint, wallpaper, and bathroom tile before the electrical was finished. So now none of the lights come on and the oven doesn't work. We had to rip off all the walls and rebuild the structure so it worked for us, and not against us. It was not fun. Do it in the right order.

Clear Information and Big Donors

Clear information affects a lot more than just the graphic design (online and on paper). It also affects your ability to get big donors.

Yes, corralling big donors is possible, even for tiny nonprofits. It's not easy, not by any means. But the methods for doing this are proven and time-tested. To cultivate big donors, our strategy had four primary components, some of which we've already covered in earlier chapters:

1) Pursue large donors, including grants

2) Run a peer-to-peer (P2P) campaign

3) Activate our network

4) Hold at least one big live event

Peer-2-peer, once again, is where you empower your supporters to go out and raise money on your behalf. So instead of the organization reaching out to people, individual supporters go to their friends, family, and coworkers and raise money from them to reach a smaller goal. When lots of people do this, it adds up to large amounts. Ideally, each supporter can set up their own fundraising web page, and this requires special software or a donor-centric CRM platform such as Salsa Labs or Classy.

Hetauda House called this our Hetauda Ambassador program.

As for our network, it had two primary sectors. First, a group of churches that people on our team already had strong pre-existing relationships with. Second, the already existing safe home program in Hetauda, Nepal, called the Women's Protection Center (WPC), which had a newsletter mailing list of about a thousand people.

But all these components – large donors, P2P, activating a network, and running a large event – depend on one crucial element, or they will never achieve their full potential. That element is clearly presented and specific information, written with donor-centric language. Let's unpack this a bit.

Trust, Clarity, and Emotion

Think about all the tasks you must perform in order to give money. Online, you have to open your wallet, type in your credit card number and all the other form fields, or pay using some online app. You have to click "Donate," or "Submit," or "Give," or some other button. Or, if paying by mail, you have to physically get your checkbook, find a pen, sit down, write out the amounts, tear off the check, put it in the envelope and seal it. Then put it in the mailbox.

What's my point? These processes can be halted at any one of these moments for all kinds of reasons, and when this happens, something deep within the person must compel them to come back and complete it later. Otherwise they never will. Online, this behavior is so commonplace it has its very own vocab term: "cart abandonment."

Donors make well-thought decisions to part with their money, knowing that if they're honest, they're not getting anything back for it. Just giving it away. It's not hard to hesitate, and ask yourself one more time if you really want to do this. How do you help donors push through this hesitation?

The number one emotion to fight off hesitancy is trust. If they don't trust you, they won't give. How do you build trust? There are lots of ways. But clarity is trust-builder #1. An unclear, vague website with scant information that looks like it was put up in a day does not provide clarity or trust.

Also, conflicting or confusing key messaging on different pages makes an organization seem, well, unorganized. Directions that don't make sense, too much jargon and acronyms, weird names for things – these sort of things make a donor scratch his chin and say, "What the heck?" Nothing dries the eyes of any remnant of empathy like jumbled jargon and bureaucratic bloviating.

One nonprofit site I visited a few years ago called the membership portion of their site an "online portal." Probably default language no one ever changed. But really? Online portal? It sounds like I'm in an old science fiction movie. That's a weird name. And I just checked again, years later. Same name is still there. How many potential subscribers (and therefore donors) has this frightening name turned away? We can only imagine.

Another nonprofit site I briefly worked with had pages and pages filled with acronyms and jargon. It read like a teacher certification handbook (don't get me started). I spent a long time looking at this site, and truly could not figure out what they do. It wasn't until I saw their LinkedIn page that I finally got it. And they were frustrated about a lack of site traffic and conversions. Hmm.

If you want big donors, you need big clarity. You need site authority. You need storytelling.

Is Good Storytelling Enough?

When it comes to fundraising, story is king.

But when it comes to a 4-pronged campaign such as ours that needs to raise a lot of money fast, story alone isn't enough. Why not?

Because information conveys credibility. And the first 3 'prongs' of our plan needed exceptional informational support to have any chance of success. Those prongs were, once again, the Ambassadors, our larger network, and big donors and grants.

Look at it this way: If you write emails and send them out to your list, your list already knows you. You have credibility. They trust you. So you can focus all your efforts on the donor, and on telling the stories you already know they want to hear.

But if you're sending out P2P fundraisers to talk to their friends and relatives who've *never heard of you*, or if you're relying on a third party (like a leader in a church in a totally different city) to present your case to their people – you need to give them enough information so they'll feel empowered and be successful. People will have questions. And they'll want answers before they give anything – especially large amounts.

To get the big donors, you need more than just stories, no matter how gut-wrenching (which the stories from Hetauda are). *Big* donors won't give just from a few emotional stories. They'll need more.

For instance, we applied for and won a $50,000 grant from a foundation that wishes to remain anonymous. Around the same time, we also applied to Construction for Change, which adopted our project. Later, we applied for several more grants, all of which denied us.

To win people like this over, we needed to be able to answer practical questions.

- How big is the house?
- What services will it provide, and to whom?
- What's the mission?

- How do we know it's safe from earthquakes?
- Is it secure?
- Who is building it?
- Can we see an itemized budget?
- Who is stewarding the funds?
- Who runs it? Do they have a track record of success?
- How will the use of our funds be correlated to data?

Large donors and foundations will have many more questions besides these, and you can't anticipate them all in advance. But you need to know how to communicate your mission and goals in such a way that a new audience gets it, feels it, and wants to be a part of it.

A story alone cannot do this. If you don't believe me, keep reading.

Real Example: Peer-2-Peer Ambassadors Need Something to Say

In our P2P strategy, the plan was to have the Ambassador show the 20 minute documentary to a group of friends and family, then go through a brief presentation and ask people to give. We created a rudimentary script people could use that included a plan for the event, suggestions on what to say and in what order, and how to close the meeting by asking for donations and if they wanted to become an Ambassador.

My wife and I tested this out on a group of 10 friends. And you need to pay attention very closely to what I'm about to describe, because this really happened, and it reveals powerful lessons and insights about fundraising.

First, these are our friends – they know us, and trust us. These were not strangers. There is no easier audience among people who don't know much about your charity. And yet, after seeing the documentary and hearing our little pitch, guess what happened?

They had questions!!

No one just opened up their wallets and threw $20 bills at us. And remember, this was immediately after a 20-minute video - stories, images, voiceovers - emotional, powerful, heartbreaking, and true accounts of life in Nepal for some women and kids.

If people we already know react with questions and not instant donations, how much more will total strangers? And yet so many websites are set up based on this vacuous assumption.

When people say all you need are stories, they're wrong. And don't misunderstand me here. I believe in using stories. They are the number one tool of fundraising. Stories get attention and draw interest. They are catalysts for action. They arouse emotion. But stories alone aren't enough.

If a 20-minute *video* story, with visuals, sound, faces, places, and all the emotion you can imagine, isn't enough to make our friends give on the spot, then that should tell us something about the necessity for additional clear information. Most people need to know something more before handing over their money. Even ten bucks, let alone tens of thousands. What they want to know will be different for each person.

But if you presume they just need a few images and stories, with maybe a few shocking statistics thrown in, and then they'll just hand over their money, prepare to be disappointed.

Information Is Power

I tell this story because if our own friends had questions, then every other Ambassador will need access to clear information so they can confidently answer questions that come up after their presentations to people even less familiar with Hetauda than our friends were. Your website and other materials aren't all just for donors. They're for the many other people who are connected to your nonprofit in some way. Knowledge is indeed power. You've got to empower your people, as well as help donors.

It should be instructive that our two $50,000 gifts (and two others in the $20k range) came in near the end of the campaign. Those people had been there the whole time. They'd known about this for months. But they gave at the end. Did something click in their minds after several months? Were they pondering whether to give, or how much, during the earlier months? When did the coin drop?

Whenever that was, it never would have happened if all we had was a single video, a few photos, and one story.

In our little Ambassador test-run with our friends, almost all their questions were answered on the website. Now it helps that I wrote the website content. But had we been average ordinary Ambassadors, the website would have been a pretty useful tool to have in that moment.

If someone asks about the budget, for example, we had a page about that. The drawings and plans for the building? We had a page about that too. Does every donor need this stuff? Of course not. But how much effort does it take for you to write it and put it up online? Not that much. And if that effort contributes to a major donor deciding to give you $50,000, will you think it was worth it?

A good website will attempt to answer the questions you know people will ask. Why wouldn't you want this to be easily available? Of course, this kind of information should not be front and center. The life-giving benefits the house will provide – the lives it will touch and how it will transform them using the donors' generous gifts – that's the story we want to tell on the home page.

But the deeper information needs to be available.

You need to empower your supporters to tell your story. They are your "brand" representatives. Your charitable work is your product. And if someone asks a friend why they give to your cause, what do you want them to say?

In that moment, they are 'pitching' a new potential donor. And the more command they have, not just of the impact you've had on the world, but of your larger mission and organization, the more compelling their case will be to their friend.

You see, people who say all we need are stories make the false assumption that getting people to give is easy. It's not easy. We showed a 20-minute story to a roomful of friends, and none of them gave that night. Not one. Weeks and months later however, several did give, and one became a very successful Ambassador. But not immediately. It took <u>follow-up</u>. It took <u>more information</u> than just one video.

Stories + Clear Information = Fundraising Success?

Remember that volunteer college student from earlier? She invited a number of her friends and their friends to hear a presentation about Hetauda. She expected at least 50 to show up, possibly over 100. And she got 8. Some of her own friends cancelled at the last minute.

After showing the video and listening to several Hetauda team members make the case, not a single person gave any money or became Ambassadors. No one wanted to use their time to raise money for impoverished kids at risk for human trafficking in Nepal. What can we say to that? I know of only one response:

Fundraising is not easy.

Here, we had stories, personal testimonies from people who've worked with WPC in various ways, terrific information, response cards and brochures – and it still didn't work.

The bottom line is – know your information well, and be ready to present it as part of a clear, organized, and compelling narrative. Don't be a bureaucrat – don't be dry and boring. But don't show up with just a smile and photos of girls in Nepal either. Not for something this big.

Just realize that being as prepared as you can possibly be, you might still fail. But without the support that comes from knowing your stuff on a deeper level than just a couple stories, failure is almost assured. You're going into battle with only one weapon and half your armor. And your team behind you will be clueless and chaotic if you falter, because all they know is the same couple of great stories you told them.

Our Success Story Is Built Upon Clearly Presented Information

There simply is no substitute for clearly presented information combined with compelling storytelling. Win over your donors with facts, impact, and emotion. If you expect to do it all with just emotion and big photos touched up by a designer, you will not reach the limits of your fundraising potential.

But there's another benefit to having clear and *easily accessible* information.

Large portions of the content I created for the website ended up re-purposed by people who didn't have time to create content. This information, written once and posted online, got used to:

- Fill out multiple grant applications
- Enhance Ambassador packets
- Market our main event
- Provide speakers with substance and taglines when they spoke to live audiences
- Create brochure content

What was the result of all this?

We had dozens of Ambassadors sign up over the months, and they raised over $35,000, collectively.

Our network responded, and raised even more. The launch event brought in over $22,000.

And best of all - we got the big donors. Construction for Change made us one of their 2016 projects. We got the $50,000 anonymous matching grant. We got another $10,000 donation later. And near the end, if you recall from chapter 1, we got two more $50,000 gifts. Without these big amounts, made possible from a continuous, clear, consistent message and call to action, Hetauda House would not have been built.

One caveat to all this: Some of this will look a little different if you run a permanent nonprofit. Ours was a one-time campaign, with a specific end-result. Once the house was funded, we were done. A permanent nonprofit will have a pre-existing structure, brand, and (hopefully) a large number of loyal supporters.

For the Hetauda House campaign, we had some of this, because the WPC Nepal program that will operate in the new safe home already exists, and has been restoring women and kids rescued from human trafficking since 2005. However, our work to raise the $500,000 to build the safe home operated independently from WPC.

So, while we had access to the key people, stories from the safe home, and their list of supporters, we were on our own for this campaign. We preferred this arrangement because it was a one-time campaign, and we didn't want to confuse or detract from the ongoing support they would still need (and still do need – if you want to support this worthy program, go to www.friendsofwpcnepal.org and give. You can even sponsor a child!).

But those differences are minor. If anything, big donors will want even more information for a permanent mission. They'll want annual reports, impact data, stories – proven effectiveness. This is even more true for grants, who are notorious for wanting all sorts of details too many organizations think they don't need because so many websites these days just have big massive photos, ten words, and a "donate now" button. As if it's that easy.

Lesson 11 Fundraising Takeaway

Back at the start, I gave you a five-step plan for what you need to do before launching a fundraising campaign. Here it is again:

1) Specify your goal
2) Create strategic plan
3) Develop core messaging and copywriting
4) Design website and materials
5) Initiate campaign

I also told you that when I came on board, Hetauda House had done only steps 1 and 4, with a few very lightly explored ideas for step 2.

In the eight months between that time and when we finally launched, we filled in the missing steps. It took a lot of time. A lot of writing, emails, and phone calls. Even an interview with Lila. A lot of meetings and planning sessions. A lot of "action items" and "to-do lists" on Trello.

But the first thing we did, before most of those meetings happened, is we had a website marketing strategy session. That's Step 2, for those of you who are counting. And from there, I created the majority of the website content we would need for the duration of the campaign. It was first-draft stuff. Some of it got updated later as we grew in our command of our own message. But that was the foundation we needed. From there, we created Ambassador packets, event materials, and all the rest.

So what's your takeaway? It's simple! **Do your fundraising in that order.**

1) Know your goal. How much are you raising? How many volunteers do you want? What's your new recurring donor goal? Find a goal for whatever you want, specify it, and then move to step 2.

2) Create a plan. What will be on the website? Who are you targeting for this? How - just online (bad idea), or also with events, direct mail, personal follow-up, or something else? What emails will you need? What print materials? Who is doing what?

3) Then you can have your copywriter and marketers get cracking, and start creating the content you'll need to execute your plan. Headlines, subject lines, calls to action, signup forms, response cards, direct mail letters or postcards - whatever you need, they will create it. Then, and only then, you are ready for step 4.

4) Have your design team take the content your writers and marketers have created, and make it presentable and usable and beautiful. If websites were a house, strategy and copywriting are the structure and layout and internal systems. Design is the paint. No one buys without paint. But no one even looks at the house if the lights don't work, the plumbing leaks, and the roof is cracked.

5) Then, you're ready to launch.

And don't forget, give your people *time* to do all these steps. Don't hand your copy and strategy to a designer and tell them to have it ready by tomorrow. People have lives.

How long does all this take? Depends on the goal. We did a Giving Tuesday campaign for another of my nonprofit clients, a very small one. It started with a clear goal – get more recurring donors. From there, we made a plan, I wrote the copy, we designed the emails and web pages, and we launched. Four weeks later, we had five new recurring givers. For that tiny nonprofit, five was a huge win. We were thrilled.

That campaign took just a few days to get through steps 1-4, and then a month to carry out. So it doesn't have to be some big huge thing. Not every goal is to raise hundreds of thousands of dollars.

But the principles are the same. Skip any of those steps, or do them in the wrong order, and you will get muddled information, confused communicators, and unmet goals.

Lesson 12

Have a Skilled Copywriter Create or Advise on All Donor Communications

WHICH IS EASIER: TO CONVINCE A BRAND NEW DONOR TO START GIVING, OR TO ask a previous donor to give again?

Do you know the answer? It's easier to ask previous donors. Then why do so many nonprofits take their current donors for granted?

Donor retention and donor cultivation far too often take a backseat to donor acquisition. And that's a tragedy, because too many nonprofits are bleeding money they could so easily be retaining. Losing a recurring giver is far more calamitous than sending out a piece of direct mail that doesn't fully recover its initial costs.

The reality is, gratitude and follow-up are quite possibly your most important fundraising tasks. And this is just one example of something you need a professional fundraising copywriter to fulfill.

The final lesson we learned in the Hetauda House campaign is just this: *You can't reach your full fundraising potential without a copywriter who specializes in this kind of writing.*

Have a Skilled Copywriter Create or Advise on All Donor Communications

Then why do organizations have secretaries and volunteers with no fundraising expertise writing thank-you emails and letters? How you thank and follow up with donors has a huge impact on whether they give again, and how much. You need someone who knows how to produce this vital fundraising content so that it preserves and deepens the donor relationship.

You may have noticed, but this book in general isn't concerned with citing statistics and research. Data is everywhere, and I've read a ton of it as part of my professional development. So if you don't know the impact that donor-follow-up marketing has on your fundraising, you can go research it on your own time. And you'll soon realize the impact is immense.

The takeaway here is very simple, but too often thrust aside in the well-meaning but usually misguided attempt to "keep costs down" - you need a professional fundraising copywriter either producing or advising on **every communication item sent to donors or potential donors**.

What does that include? Any of the following, and probably more:

- Email newsletters to whole or partial lists
- Email autoresponders to newsletter signups - a welcome series is ideal. Do NOT send an automated email filled with techno-gibberish. We are not computers.
- Email autoresponders thanking anyone who gives
- Email autoresponders for any other online action, such as signing up to be a volunteer or a p2p fundraiser
- Direct mail fundraising letters and postcards
- Direct mail thank you letters
- Website content - all main pages
- Donation pages - if your donation page only has fields to fill out, you are missing out on donations. Message reinforcement is critical at any point a person has to type in a credit card number.
- Landing pages for any external ads or links from elsewhere on the site, or links given on direct mail items.

- External online ads, such as Adwords (or Adgrants)
- Facebook and other social media marketing copy
- Unique methods of thanking large donors (ideally this should also include personal contact by phone or in person, depending on their preference)
- Blog content
- Event promotional and marketing copy
- All printed items like brochures, response cards, handouts – you need walk-away items to give people anytime you do anything in person. Send your people in empty-handed, and they'll come back empty-handed.

I'm sure there's more, but you get the idea. There's a lot to be written that donors will see. If you have a small staff, you know it's impossible for one person to do all (or even part) of this in a reasonable amount of time.

But if you have just one professional copywriter, even on a contract basis, who can put his eyes on all this stuff even if he isn't the one creating it, your fundraising impact will enlarge.

For some of my clients, this happens a lot. In one recent experience, I was hired primarily to write emails. But one day they sent me a direct mail letter that someone else (not a copywriter) wrote as a first draft. They don't want to pay me to write it from scratch (which I understand), but they want me to revise it for a lower fee. So they still got the higher quality copy, but at a level they can manage.

Unexpected needs for new writing will arise suddenly, and you need a copywriter on hand who can address them quickly.

With Hetauda, we realized about midway through the campaign that our Ambassadors were starting to lag a bit. Many had stopped raising money, and many hadn't raised any at all. We were concerned new ones might come on and not really know where to start.

So, we sat down and planned out a 10-email Ambassador "motivational" on-boarding series. We gave tips and strategies for how to raise money and identify their networks. Five of the ten emails were testimonials – stories of successful Ambassadors who had all raised over $1000 already.

The point was to give practical ideas and strategies and mix it in with real success stories so people would feel encouraged that yes, this can be done, and I can do it.

I wrote the full series and we sent it out to all the new Ambassadors from that point on. In our case, since our campaign ended a few months later, the effects of that series were hard to measure.

However, if you have an ongoing p2p program and do not have an appropriate on-boarding series like this, now you've got another idea to add to your list. The confidence this will give your new p2p fundraisers will be substantial. And the great thing about an autoresponder series like this is, you only have to write it once.

Why You Need a Copywriting Specialist

If you look at just two components of your organization – your staff and your schedule – your need for a copywriter should be as obvious as our need for food, water, and sunlight. Your staff is overworked, and your schedule is overbooked. A copywriter reduces the workload for your staff, and frees up their schedules so they can get more done in less time.

Here's a list to elaborate on what a copywriter does to move your mission forward with greater effectiveness and efficiency:

1) Ability to handle urgent writing assignments

I just gave one such example. For a ten month campaign already in month five, if we're going to get any value at all out of an Ambassador on-boarding email series, we need to get it written fast, and written well. We want its recipients to be grateful for how helpful it is, and not annoyed at having their time wasted.

Writing needs like this can come up with little warning, like a storm on the ocean. Having someone within reach who already knows your organization, your mission, and your core messaging, and who can produce what you need quickly without sacrificing quality, is immensely valuable.

It also leads to the second reason to have a copywriter:

2) Remove the burden and pressure of writing from your staff

Your staff hates writing copy. Trust me, they do. I've heard it over and over. They'll pay someone to set up a website. They'll coordinate volunteers. Plan meetings. Take notes. Call people up. They'll even suggest strategy ideas and help out at events.

But they hate writing the copy. Especially the stuff the donors will see. You know, those scary, intimidating people who are the lifeblood of your mission. The ones with the checkbooks with padlocks on all four sides, and each key is buried deep underwater in a lake inside separate combination lock safes. Inside a metal cage surrounded by piranhas.

Seriously though. People get nervous writing things they know will be judged. And copywriting has to face the music every time it gets sent out. Someone will read it. They might not like it. They might even get annoyed and unsubscribe from your list. Worst of all, they might catch that typo you missed and scoff about it!

Your staff hates writing copy. And that's why most nonprofits, especially small ones, have terrible copywriting. Because no one wants to do it! But that's not the only reason. And in rare exceptions, you might have a staff person who likes writing. But...

3) Your staff doesn't have time to write

Every nonprofit staff is overworked, underpaid, and never has enough time. There are fires to put out, people who need to be called, reports to write, and so much more. And let's not forget the reason you're all here in the first place - you want to help fix something that's broken in the world! So if anything arises that concerns the people (or animals) your nonprofit exists to help, you'll drop everything to go meet the need. As you should.

Have a Skilled Copywriter Create or Advise on All Donor Communications

But what gets dropped anytime the stress piles up? Anything that can be put off until later. And what can almost always be put off? The writing.

The result of this is that the writing gets done, if at all, at the last minute. With little thought put into all the details that matter. Like the headline. The opening. The call to action. The structure. The theme that ties it all together. How it relates to the other channels of your marketing. How your donors will perceive it.

Details get missed. Sloppiness invades. Your supporters end up getting emails about events with last year's location, matching grant deadlines with the wrong date, and a letter signed by your CEO when it's supposed to be from one of the girls your charity has helped. Oops.

When you produce last-minute thrown-together content, it does not impact your audience the way it needs to. Achieving that kind of impact takes time and focus. Something your staff simply doesn't have.

4) Obsessive and Single-Minded Fixation

How many tasks does your project manager have to perform? Can you count that high? You can't, because it changes every day. How about your secretary, or HR director? What about your case workers, or even your fundraising director?

They all have tons of things to do. Too much.

But a copywriter has just one thing to do. Write copy. It's the one thing no one else wants to do or has time to do, and when they do it, their minds are in 20 different places.

You want a writer who focuses *just on writing*, without worrying about all that other stuff. You want a writer who has the time to obsess about your message, your audience, your donors, and the best ways to get, hold, and capitalize on their attention and concern for your mission.

In other words, you want someone you can just hand stuff to, and say "please get this done." And a little while later, it's done! A thank you email? A direct mail revision? A new landing page? An update to the home page? Done.

More and more companies and nonprofits are starting to do this with tech-related tasks. They contract out website work and tech improvements and adjustments. But too many nonprofits still don't do this with the single most important component of their fundraising strategy - their messaging.

Find a trusted and professional copywriter, hand your stuff to them, and then get back to the other thirty items on your list.

5) You'll get more donors!

This is the most obvious reason to have a professional copywriter on hand, but I don't want you to overlook it.

None of the great things you want to accomplish will happen without donors. We all understand this in our heads. But very often the application of that knowledge doesn't reach our hands.

You need more donors, more money, more supporters, and more volunteers. We all do.

From the smallest nonprofit getting by on a few thousand a month, to the huge one that's nationwide or worldwide, to the brand new startup with almost nothing - you need donors. To get donors, you need a message and a way to communicate that to the right people.

You won't figure out how to do this without someone who does it for a living.

Now, the smaller nonprofits are probably thinking, "Yes, but we can't afford it." The good news is, this actually isn't true.

I've done work for what qualifies as a "startup" nonprofit. They do outreach to homeless people, and have a unique approach and philosophy that sets them apart from all the other homeless ministries.

When I came to work for this group, guess how many donors they had? (Hint: it starts with a 'Z'). That's right - they had zero donors. Not a one. No donors means no money, right? Actually, no. The founder of this ministry cares so much about helping the homeless get off the streets that he invests (key word) his own money in his program.

He also got one large 'seed' donation that helped kick things off. So they had some money. Enough to hire me to re-write their nearly incomprehensible website, among other things. Since then, they hired me to write a few emails and blogs throughout the year. Again, they're not paying me much, but the important thing is – they are investing in what they know will pay off.

Every nonprofit has to have money somewhere, or they would cease to exist. For this homeless ministry, he's investing his own money because he understands that's the only way to grow. It's not going to just "happen." You have to invest if you want to grow.

So how's it working out?

As of this writing, they are bringing in nearly $800 per month in recurring and one-time donations, and I've only been actively fundraising for them for about a year. Was his investment worth it?

A professional copywriter in fundraising understands that different organizations are at different places. Just like you do your work because you want to help solve some problem in the world, a fundraising copywriter wants the same thing!

I know there are plenty of other ways to earn money through copywriting. But I want to write for nonprofits because I want to do something about the suffering in this world. Same as you. So I understand that smaller organizations can't pay as much, and I can adjust my fees accordingly. The important thing is growth and impact.

In other words, professional doesn't have to mean expensive.

It just means you'll get your money's worth, and will have a productive and healthy collaboration in the process.

If your secretary is writing your email newsletters, you are losing donations. If your daughter the English major is editing your direct mail letters, you are losing donations (for sure). If your graphic designer is the one deciding what to put on your website, you are most definitely losing donations.

Do you want more donors? Then you want a fundraising copywriter.

Fine. But How Do I Find a Fundraising Copywriter?

This all depends on how hard you're willing to look, and how much time you have.

There are plenty of online places to advertise for contract (freelance) work. You might be surprised at the quality of people you can find on there.

Another great option is to reach out to organizations that train copywriters. In my case, my initial training came through a program called AWAI. It's a robust copywriting training program, all led by professional copywriters who have been very successful in hundreds of industries. They have special courses in every form of copywriting there is, from B2B to information marketing to email to SEO to content marketing, and everything in between.

If you reach out to them (or post an ad on their jobs page), you'll get responses, and you can be confident their students will be better on average than someone you'll find on random websites like Craig's List. If you want the best, you go where copywriters are.

You can also just do web searches and see what comes up. There are plenty of fundraising copywriters who have their own sites. These are probably even better options than AWAI, because you already know they specialize in your field. Specialization in fundraising is really important because it's a different type of copywriting than traditional marketing copy. Some principles are the same, but the audience expectations are very different, as are some of the more advanced strategies only specialists who continually educate themselves will know.

But your simplest option is, not to be too blunt about it, already right in front of you. You've read my story. You already have a clear picture of what I can do, my expertise and experience, and what you can expect when working with me. You know my commitment, passion, and concern for your mission and that you'll get a measurable impact from my work.

If you are interested in working with me and have read this far into the book, there's a special offer available at the end of this chapter that you are free to take advantage of.

Your Lesson 12 Fundraising Takeaway is to go read that offer and act on it.

How Can I Tell if a Copywriter Is Actually Any Good?

This is a harder question to answer. The reason is because even the best copywriters in the world have written stuff that bombed. No one bats a thousand. No one wins them all.

So basing expertise on results - while that is certainly an important factor - can't be your only criteria. Plus, there are always other factors in play in any successful campaign. I did not make Hetauda happen on my own. Not even close.

The best way to detect and confirm expertise is to ask the right questions. Here are a few questions you can ask a copywriter you're thinking of hiring:

1) What do you think makes for a successful p2p campaign?

I like this question because it uses jargon. In fundraising, jargon is a terrible idea. But if you're hiring a fundraising specialist, they should know what p2p means. And you know what it means, because I explained it earlier in this book. This is a simple test to first see if they even know the term.

The rest of their answer doesn't really matter that much, as long as it's clear they know what peer-to-peer fundraising is and have worked on campaigns that utilized it with some success.

2) Tell me about a fundraising event you helped promote.

When I say "promote," I mean market. Now, they may have also done some volunteering at events and learned a few things that way (which is not insignificant, by the way - any more than it is for a trade apprentice to learn by watching a master). But ideally, you want a writer who has written marketing copy for fundraising events. Could be emails, fliers, auction donation letters, direct mail, magazine ads, even TV commercials.

Do they know how to promote events and get people to attend? Here, someone who's marketed for-profit events may be more valuable than a fundraising copywriter who's never attended or marketed an event. Events are unique, as I indicated in Lesson #7, and it's a unique skillset that knows how to promote them too. Personally, I've done both types.

But if your copywriter has no event experience, but has lots of other fundraising marketing expertise, they might still be a good person to work with. They can learn about event marketing over time, and eventually contribute in that area as well.

But a "good" fundraising copywriter should have some knowledge of and hopefully experience with event marketing.

    3) What do you think is the most effective way to raise money?

Here, there is no right answer. However, there are many wrong ones. If they say "crowdfunding" for example, run for the hills. But really, you're asking this question just to get them talking. You can tell someone knows something if they can talk about it off the cuff for ten minutes without needing any prompts. I think this is a broad enough question that a fundraising expert should have a lot to say about it.

And their first line will probably be something like, "There isn't one most effective way, or everyone would be doing it." That's the sign of a fundraising expert. They might also say, "Keep the focus on the donor, not the organization." If they say that, that's a good sign.

But, that question is also broad enough that a non-copywriter who has fundraising experience in a different role might still be able to sneak in a nice-sounding answer. That's why you need question 4.

    4) Describe your copywriting process.

Have a Skilled Copywriter Create or Advise on All Donor Communications

Here, you're looking for specifics. If the first thing they do is sit down and write a first draft, they are not a good copywriter. A professional copywriter never writes a draft as their FIRST step.

There's a lot to figure out before you get to that point. What's the goal of this campaign? What are we asking people to do (call to action)? Who's this being sent to, and why them? Have these people seen anything before, and if so, how long ago?

An expert copywriter will also talk about the message. Can we tell a story? They also won't fixate only on positive stories. Sometimes, you want stories with unhappy endings too. Why? Because those stories show people there's an immediate need they can meet. They might also talk about the structure of a letter or email, or a multi-pronged strategy and how their writing will fit into it.

We could go on for a while here, and there isn't only one process. But you're looking for someone who *has* a process, who knows the questions they need to ask, and what they do with those once they have the answers.

For me, I have a four-step general process: Ask, Understand, Recommend, Create. Under each of those is a list of more specific details. Sometimes they are job-specific, sometimes not. But the important thing is, notice where "create" sits. At the end. I don't start writing until a lot of other work has been done before.

The good news is, once your copywriter knows your organization well, their process will get faster. I can write for Friends of WPC Nepal (the program that uses the Hetauda House building) very quickly because I know their mission inside and out.

    5) Can you give us some examples of successes and failures?

It's good to ask for both. Why? Because everyone has failures. With those, you want to know what they learned from them. But if they have no successes, that might be a red flag. And remember, even a brand new writer can still be a fundraising specialist if they've gotten good training and continue educating themselves. You might pay them a lower rate, but they can still do great work for you.

So if they are a new writer, but have answered your other questions well enough, go ahead and take a chance on them.

But ideally, they would have some successes under their belt, and should be able to talk confidently about them. And you want specific numbers here. Not, "we grew a lot that year." No, you want something like, "I wrote a 4-email series, and it produced a 360% ROI." And then ask them for specifics of why they think that campaign was a success.

Remember, this is a copywriter. Not a department head. The copywriter writes discreet items that are trackable in most cases. They should have numbers.

There are other questions you could ask, but the main thing is to get them talking and feel like you learned something by listening to them.

Notice what I didn't ask here:

How many years of experience do you have? Do you have a marketing degree (totally irrelevant)? Can we see some of your samples? If they've answered these other questions well, you don't need to waste everyone's time with samples. Professionals are sick of samples. We don't need to prove to non-writers that we know how to write. How would a non-writer know what quality *fundraising copywriting* looks like anyway?

Do you have any references? That's not necessarily a bad question, but if they have a website, it should have a few testimonials on it. If you really want to take the time to call references, feel free. But since this is contract work, it's just not that important. If you don't like their work after a few projects, then just end it.

Why Your Fundraising Director Is Not a Copywriter

As a final point about copywriting, I want to distinguish these two roles. Some of this is probably just a grudge I have to get over, because I've been turned down for work at a few organizations because they already have a "fundraising director."

You need to understand the difference here, because these are not the same role.

Have a Skilled Copywriter Create or Advise on All Donor Communications

The director role is like a marketing manager at a business. This person is a department head. An overseer. A supervisor. This person has a lot of tasks on their plate.

It was actually with the fundraising director in mind that I compiled the earlier list of reasons why you need a fundraising copywriter. The director is overworked, doesn't have time to write quality copy, is too busy with other tasks, and won't be able to produce content in a hurry.

Fundraising directors do a lot more than just write copy. They interact with donors and create plans for strengthening those relationships. They provide long term vision and strategy. They reach out to the community for support. They plan logistics for events. They work with major donors and businesses. They do much more than this short list.

But they do not have time to sit down for three hours and write an email series. The proper role of the director is as the supervisor for the copywriter. The writer produces the content, and the director evaluates it and offer revisions that the copywriter goes back and implements.

These two will work together. And while it's possible a fundraising director might have copywriting skills from prior experience, in the director role they don't have time to focus on that to the degree it requires. Remember – *obsessive focus* on writing produces better results. Your director cannot do this. If you try to force this because you don't want to invest in a copywriter, two things will happen:

1) Your donations won't grow as much as you hoped, if at all

2) You won't produce nearly as much fundraising content as you need

And a third thing might happen after that: Your fundraising director will quit. There is a lot of turnover in this position. Why? Because it's a big job. Too big a job to also expect them to write the copy.

Lesson 12 Fundraising Takeaway

This one's pretty simple. Go find a copywriter or two. Then interview them using the five questions I gave you. You're looking for someone who can both strategize and implement. If your copywriter completely depends on others to come up with ideas, then now your fundraising director has yet another task to worry about.

The copywriter should also be a strategist and have a consultant's approach to the job. That way, the writer becomes an asset to the director, and not a burden. The copywriter should make the director's job easier and more effective, not harder and more stressful.

One important caveat – and this is above and beyond the interview questions. Make sure your copywriter will be able to get along with your team and aligns with your values. It doesn't make much sense for a writer who loves burgers, ribs, and meat-lovers pizzas to write fundraising copy for a vegan nonprofit. Nor for a Christian copywriter to write for an abortion-rights nonprofit, or a gun-control advocate to write for a 2nd amendment organization.

These things should be obvious.

Less obvious might be something like this: If your work concerns helping poor people in India, don't hire a copywriter who doesn't really care about global poverty. Sure, that writer can work himself or herself up to the task and figure out what your donors care about, and all the other issues that go along. But it really matters that your writer can share some of the passion and emotion for your cause.

After all, the whole point of your copy is to arouse emotions like anger, compassion, and empathy in your donors – who also care about your cause.

There's nothing wrong at all with screening your copywriter to see if their values and passions are a good match for your own.

Me? I tend to focus mostly on human services nonprofits. Animals are great, but I don't get as passionate about the charities that rescue and protect animals like other people do. I could write for them if I was hired to do so, but I wouldn't go out of my way to do so.

But global or local poverty, disaster relief, injustice, education, homelessness – these are the sorts of things I tend to gravitate toward.

Have a Skilled Copywriter Create or Advise on All Donor Communications

Every writer has their passions, interests, and preferences. Ideally, you will find an expert one who shares some of yours. Another way to tell if your writer shares your values – will writing for your charity feel like a job, or an honor? For me, Hetauda was one of the greatest honors of my life.

Jobs are easy to quit. But if it's an honor for them to work for you, they'll likely stick with you as long as they possibly can. And that loyalty pays off in countless ways as they gain more institutional knowledge about your work.

Final Thoughts on the Hetauda House Building Project

I AM VERY HAPPY TO HAVE BEEN A PART OF THIS PROJECT. IT WAS EXTREMELY hard work, and it wore us down pretty low a few times.

But when I saw the first photos of the new foundation for the building, it was quite an experience. My emotions swelled as they rarely do. This house is going to be a sanctuary for hundreds of women and kids in the coming years. We have created something that won't just transform a few people's lives. It very well could transform the whole nation of Nepal. I've included a few photos of the building being constructed at the end of the book.

The girls and boys growing up in the safety, love, and provision in the WPC Nepal safe home known as Hetauda House are going to graduate from high school and go on to do things with their lives that were not just impossible before. They will do things - nation-strengthening things like building strong families and getting jobs that improve life for their towns and cities - that will resonate for decades, and ripple across cities and other families.

Already, human traffickers have been cowed into the shadows because of WPC Nepal's effects on the community. WPC doesn't just help the kids in their home. They go out and teach people how to recognize traffickers. How to discern when they're being lied to about where this man says he will take their son or daughter. They even go into schools and teach it to the kids directly.

I heard one story from Lila, the founder of WPC Nepal, that encapsulates this cultural effect perfectly.

It happened when the group of men from the U.S. went to lay the groundwork for what is now becoming the Hetauda House. One day, a woman came out to try to sell a girl to them. The girl was her own daughter. Yes, this really happens. It's horrific to imagine.

This mother has clearly done this before, and when she saw the westerners approaching, she assumed something about them. Something that wasn't true for these particular men. But something that is, very disturbingly, true for many others who come to nations like Nepal. (And the fact this is true puts a dark light on the notion that our country is somehow "great", by the way. "Sexual tourism" is a real thing. And the "tourists" don't come from Antarctica. They come from your city. Nothing great about that).

So this woman was coming out to prostitute her own offspring. But then, she saw Lila with them. And at the mere sight of Lila, she ran back into her house with her daughter. No sale.

Lila's very presence represents a cultural shift for her people. That we will not stand for abuse, exploitation, or the sale of our women and children any longer. That change is possible.

That story tells me that her message is getting out.

The new 5-story Hetauda House will stand above many of the buildings in the city. What it stands for is freedom, hope, dignity, worth, and value – a chance to live a life free from the control of greedy and dehumanized men and women who will do anything to make more money for themselves. A chance to rebuild their nation on a different kind of foundation that doesn't devalue girls or people from low castes.

Hetauda House is a monument to hope for a new future for Nepal. Projects like this are why people like me do what we do. I hope you've enjoyed reading the lessons learned along the way, but I wanted to end with this, because this is why all that other stuff matters.

We're not doing this work to build a nest egg for ourselves. We're not doing this work just because our organizations need the money. We're doing it to build something that lasts forever – for the souls of people in need who too often have no one else on their side.

Final Thoughts on the Hetauda House Building Project

The Ultimate Fundraising Case Study

Final Thoughts on the Hetauda House Building Project

Final Thoughts on the Hetauda House Building Project

Special Fundraising Opportunity

Do you want to grow your donations? Get more recurring donors? Deepen the loyalty of your supporters? I'm guessing you do, because what you really want is to see your mission succeed and impact the world to make it better.

As a fundraising copywriter, I share your passion to change the world. I don't buy the cynicism peddled by many today. Change is possible, and there are a lot of people who want to see it happen and who will give their time, money, and hearts to make it so.

Because you've read this book, I have a special opportunity to share with you.

Work with me as your go-to fundraising copywriter, and I will give you $500 of free copywriting. No strings attached. All you have to do is contact me through my website:

proactivecontent.net/bookoffer

When you send me a message, just say "I read your book" and tell me **one thing you really liked about it or learned from it,** and you will get a $500 advance on any copywriting you want me to create for you.

What can you get for $500 of free copywriting?

Quite a lot, actually. A new autoresponder email series? How about newsletters – printed or emailed? You can get blog posts, new web page content, thank you letters, event consultation and promotion – there's quite a variety, and I can't really give you specifics because it depends on what you need.

This is a blank check, and in the memo it says "copywriting." So once we connect and talk about your organization and its needs, you'll get your first $500 of writing free.

I don't think there's a single fundraising copywriter on this planet who would give a deal this good. But I'm doing it because I want to help you accomplish your mission to change the world and make it better for the people living in it now, and in the future.

The Ultimate Fundraising Case Study

Final Thoughts on the Hetauda House Building Project